Bloom's
GUIDES

Sophocles'
Oedipus Rex

CURRENTLY AVAILABLE

The Adventures of Huckleberry
  Finn
All the Pretty Horses
Animal Farm
Beloved
Beowulf
Brave New World
The Catcher in the Rye
The Chosen
The Crucible
Cry, the Beloved Country
Death of a Salesman
Fahrenheit 451
Frankenstein
The Glass Menagerie
The Grapes of Wrath
Great Expectations
The Great Gatsby
Hamlet
The Handmaid's Tale
The House on Mango Street
I Know Why the Caged Bird Sings
The Iliad
Jane Eyre

Lord of the Flies
Macbeth
Maggie: A Girl of the Streets
The Member of the Wedding
The Metamorphosis
Native Son
Of Mice and Men
1984
The Odyssey
Oedipus Rex
One Hundred Years of Solitude
Pride and Prejudice
Ragtime
The Red Badge of Courage
Romeo and Juliet
Slaughterhouse-Five
The Scarlet Letter
Snow Falling on Cedars
A Streetcar Named Desire
The Sun Also Rises
A Tale of Two Cities
The Things They Carried
To Kill a Mockingbird
The Waste Land

Bloom's

GUIDES

Sophocles'
Oedipus Rex

Edited & with an Introduction
by Harold Bloom

BLOOM'S
LITERARY CRITICISM
An imprint of Infobase Publishing

Bloom's Guides: Oedipus Rex

Copyright © 2007 by Infobase Publishing

Introduction © 2007 by Harold Bloom

All rights reserved. No part of this book may be reproduced or utilized in any form or by any means, electronic or mechanical, including photocopying, recording, or by any information storage or retrieval systems, without permission in writing from the publisher. For information contact:

Bloom's Literary Criticism
An imprint of Infobase Publishing
132 West 31st Street
New York NY 10001

Library of Congress Cataloging-in-Publication Data
Sophocles' Oedipus rex / [edited by] Harold Bloom.
    p. cm. — (Bloom's guides)
  Includes bibliographical references and index.
  ISBN-13: 978-0-7910-9360-3
  ISBN-10: 0-7910-9360-3
  1. Sophocles. Oedipus Rex. 2. Oedipus (Greek mythology) in literature.
I. Bloom, Harold. II. Title. III. Series.

  PA4413.O7S663 2007
  882'.01—dc22   2007010028

Bloom's Literary Criticism books are available at special discounts when purchased in bulk quantities for businesses, associations, institutions, or sales promotions. Please call our Special Sales Department in New York at (212) 967-8800 or (800) 322-8755.

You can find Bloom's Literary Criticism on the World Wide Web at
http://www.chelseahouse.com

Contributing Editor: Camille-Yvette Welsch
Cover design by Takeshi Takahashi
Printed in the United States of America
Bang EJB 10 9 8 7 6 5 4 3 2 1
This book is printed on acid-free paper.

All links and web addresses were checked and verified to be correct at the time of publication. Because of the dynamic nature of the web, some addresses and links may have changed since publication and may no longer be valid.

Contents

Introduction

HAROLD BLOOM

Whether there is a "tragic flaw," a *hamartia*, in King Oedipus is uncertain, though I doubt it, as he is hardly a figure who shoots wide of the mark. Accuracy is implicit in his nature. We can be certain that he is free of that masterpiece of ambivalence—Freud's Oedipal complex. In the Age of Freud, we are uncertain what to do with a guiltless Oedipus, but that does appear to be the condition of Sophocles' hero. We cannot read *Oedipus the King* as we read the *Iliad* of Homer, where the gods matter enormously. And even more, we know it is absurd to read *Oedipus* as though it were written by the Yahwist, or the authors of Jeremiah or Job, let alone of the Gospels. We can complete our obstacle course by warning ourselves not to compound *Oedipus* with *Hamlet* or *Lear*. Homer and the Bible, Shakespeare and Freud, teach us only how not to read Sophocles.

When I was younger, I was persuaded by Cedric Whitman's eloquent book on Sophocles to read *Oedipus* as a tragedy of "heroic humanism." I am not so persuaded now, not because I am less attracted by a humanistic heroism, but because I am uncertain how such a stance allows for tragedy. William Blake's humanism was more than heroic, being apocalyptic, but it too would not authorize tragedy. However the meaning of *Oedipus* is to be interpreted in our post-Nietzchean age, the play is surely tragedy, or the genre will lose coherence. E. R. Dodds, perhaps assimilating Sophocles to the *Iliad*, supposed that the tragedy of Oedipus honored the gods, without judging them to be benign or even just. Bernard Knox argues that the greatness of the gods and the greatness of Oedipus are irreconcilable, with tragedy the result of that schism. That reduces to the Hegelian view of tragedy as an agon between right and right, but Knox gives the preference to Oedipus, since the gods, being ever victorious, therefore cannot be heroic. A less Homeric reading than Dodds's, this seems to me too much our sense of heroism—Malraux perhaps, rather than Sophocles.

Freud charmingly attributed to Sophocles, as a precursor of psychoanalysis, the ability to have made possible a self–analysis for the playgoer. But then Freud called *Oedipus* an "immoral play," since the gods ordained incest and patricide. Oedipus therefore participates in our universal unconscious sense of guilt, but on this reading so do the gods. I sometimes wish that Freud had turned to Aeschylus instead, and given us the Prometheus complex rather than the Oedipus complex. Plato is Oedipal in regard to Homer, but Sophocles is not. I hardly think that Sophocles would have chastised Homer for impiety, but then, as I read it, the tragedy of Oedipus takes up no more skeptical stance than that of Plato, unless one interprets Plato as Montaigne wished to interpret him.

What does any discerning reader remember most vividly about *Oedipus the King*? Almost certainly, the answer must be the scene of the king's self–blinding, as narrated by the second messenger, here in David Grene's version:

By her own hand. The worst of what was done
you cannot know. You did not see the sight.
Yet in so far as I remember it
you'll hear the end of our unlucky queen.
When she came raging into the house she went
straight to her marriage bed, tearing her hair
with both her hands, and crying upon Laius
long dead—Do you remember, Laius,
that night long past which bred a child for us
to send you to your death and leave
a mother making children with her son?
And then she groaned and cursed the bed in which
she brought forth husband by her husband, children
by her own child, an infamous double bond.
How after that she died I do not know,—
for Oedipus distracted us from seeing.
He burst upon us shouting and we looked
to him as he paced frantically around,

begging us always: Give me a sword, I say,
to find this wife no wife, this mother's womb,
this field of double sowing whence I sprang
and where I sowed my children! As he raved
some god showed him the way—none of us there.
Bellowing terribly and led by some
invisible guide he rushed on the two doors, —
wrenching the hollow bolts out of their sockets,
he charges inside. There, there, we saw his wife
hanging, the twisted rope around her neck.
When he saw her, he cried out fearfully
and cut loose the dangling noose. Then, as she lay,
poor woman, on the ground, what happened after,
was terrible to see. He tore the brooches—
the gold chased brooches fastening her robe—
away from her and lifting them high
dashed them on his own eyeballs, shrieking out
such things as: they will never see the crime
I have committed or had done upon me!
Dark eyes, now on the days to come, look on
forbidden faces, do not recognize
those whom you long for—with such imprecations
he struck his eyes again and yet again
with the brooches. And the bleeding eyeballs gushed
and stained his beard—no sluggish oozing drops
but a black rain and bloody hail poured down.
So it has broken—and not on one head
but troubles mixed for husband and wife.
The fortune of the days gone by was true
good fortune—but today groans and destruction
and death and shame—of all ills can be named
not one is missing.
(1.1237–86)

The scene, too terrible for acting out, seems also too
dreadful for representation in language. Oedipus, desiring
to put a sword in the womb of Jocasta, is led by "some god"
to where he can break through the two doors (I shudder as

I remember Walt Whitman's beautiful trope for watching a woman in childbirth, "I recline by the sills of the exquisite flexible doors"). Fortunately finding Jocasta self–slain, lest he add the crime of matricide to patricide and incest, Oedipus, repeatedly stabbing his eyes with Jocasta's brooches, passes judgment not so much upon seeing as upon the seen, and so upon the light by which we see. I interpret this as his protest against Apollo, which brings both the light and the plague. The Freudian trope of blinding for castration seems to me less relevant here than the outcry against the god.

To protest Apollo is necessarily dialectical, since the pride and agility of the intellect of Oedipus, remorselessly searching out the truth, in some sense is also against the nature of truth. In this vision of reality, you shall know the truth, and the truth will make you mad. What would make Oedipus free? Nothing that happens in this play, must be the answer, nor does it seem that becoming an oracular god later on makes you free either. If you cannot be free of the gods, then you cannot be made free, and even acting as though your daemon is your destiny will not help you either.

The startling ignorance of Oedipus when the drama begins is the *given* of the play, and cannot be questioned or disallowed. Voltaire was scathing upon this, but the ignorance of the wise and the learned remains an ancient truth of psychology, and torments us every day. I surmise that this is the true force of Freud's Oedipus complex: not the unconscious sense of guilt, but the necessity of ignorance, lest the reality–principle destroy us. Nietzsche said it not in praise of art, but so as to indicate the essential limitation of art. Sophoclean irony is more eloquent yet:

CREON: Do not seek to be master in everything, for the things you mastered did not follow you throughout your life.

(*As Creon and Oedipus go out.*)

CHORUS: You that live in my ancestral Thebes, behold this Oedipus,—him who knew the famous riddles

and was a man most masterful; not a citizen who
did not look with envy on his lot—see him now
and see the breakers of misfortune swallow him!
Look upon that last day always. Count no mortal
happy till he has passed the final limit of his life secure from pain.

Biographical Sketch

Seven plays of Sophocles have survived for twenty-four centuries. The great ideas that he dramatized with such energy and poetry embrace or transcend many of the important issues that successive generations of artists have struggled to comprehend and express. His work continues to be compelling and fully relevant.

It is unfortunate that so little is known about the poet's life and nothing is known to account for what inspired him to dramatize so many stories about the anguish and mystery of human life. Even his birth and death dates are inexact (497/496 B.C.–406/405 B.C.). We do know that his life in Athens—spanning almost all of the fifth century B.C.—roughly overlapped a period of great cultural activity culminating in the establishment of Athenian democracy. One source of biographical information is an anonymous *Life*, found in Paris in a thirteenth-century manuscript of the plays. Among the facts generally accepted as reliable are his place of birth in the section of Athens known as "Colonus"—a mile north of the Acropolis, said to be the burial site of Oedipus—and his birth into a wealthy and established family. He was accomplished in music, poetry, and wrestling. From his two marriages came five sons, one of whom—Iophon—was also a tragic poet. Sophocles' grandson produced *Oedipus at Colonus* after his grandfather's death. Among other random interesting facts is a report of Sophocles' prominent role in a public celebration of Athens's second defeat of the Persian invaders in 480 B.C. He was chosen to lead the victory dance because of his charm and handsome bearing.

The form of drama known as Greek tragedy is closely associated with the culture of Athens. With its high regard for the competitive spirit, the city organized public festivals where artists competed for prizes for the best tragic plays. The festivals were held to honor Dionysus, a Thracian deity associated with revelry, who eventually became the god of wine, theater, and merrymaking in Greek mythology. In 468 B.C.,

Sophocles gained instant fame by winning his first competition, beating Aeschylus, a generation older and his nearest rival. He also competed (and won) in competition with Euripides. For a period of time, Sophocles followed the tradition of poets acting in their own plays, but his voice was considered "weak" and he had to desist. In his lifetime, Sophocles won twenty victories, never, it is claimed, placing lower than second. Three plays were required for a single presentation so his twenty victories represented an outstanding achievement. He went on to write more than 120 plays (most have been lost), two satyr plays, and miscellaneous fragments. He was an acclaimed artist for the duration of his life.

Since so little biographical material is available, scholars have looked to the plays for evidence of Sophocles' concerns and interests. We know that in common with generations of students, Sophocles read Homer's *Odyssey*; much of his material originates with Homer and other ancient myths. His heroine Antigone has become associated with principled resistance to state power and reverence for the dignity of personal loyalties. The influence of Sophism, an intellectual and philosophical movement in Sophocles' time that encouraged the use of persuasive reasoning to challenge old ways of thinking, is represented in the character of Creon in *Oedipus Rex*. Creon uses Sophist reasoning to dissuade Oedipus from believing that he wants to retake the crown of Thebes. Creon's reasoning in this scene is persuasive, but other scenes and the general impact of the play on audiences suggest that Sophocles regarded rational thinking an inadequate explanation for human behavior. Many scholars believe that Sophocles was challenging the intellectual minds of his time in these scenes. For all the sensibleness of Creon's reasoning—especially in contrast to the emotional excesses of Oedipus in those same scenes— Creon seems to many the less interesting and certainly the less memorable of the two characters.

An important clue about Sophocles' beliefs can be deduced from what the playwright leaves out. Although known to be a religious man Sophocles uses no supernatural tricks or the literary device *deus ex machina* to solve a conundrum in the plot or produce a contrived conclusion. Sophocles' story lines and outcomes—although arresting and spectacular—evolve from character and believable human impulses.

In the historical background of Sophocles' life are the Persian invasions of Athens (unsuccessful until after his death) and the reign of Pericles over the cultural and military rise of Athens. In addition to being a celebrated poet, Sophocles served the public interest, occupying a number of high public offices. In 443–2 Sophocles' name appears on the inscribed tribute lists as a Hellenotamias, a position akin to that of minister of finance. Under Pericles he was twice a general, a position less engaged in military affairs than in policy decisions and management of resources.

Sophocles lived to age ninety or ninety-one. One speculation about the cause of death is his exultation at a public reading of *Antigone*, but no details are certain. He lived to a good old age. All accounts of his life describe Sophocles as a kind and gentle man, full of charm and well loved by many. At the time of his death, Athens was under siege from Sparta, but a break in hostilities was arranged to make possible the proper burial of an esteemed citizen.

The comic dramatist Phrynichus wrote in *Muses* (405 B.C.):

Blest is Sophocles who lived a long life and died a happy
and accomplished man: he wrote many excellent tragedies
and died a good death, having suffered no troubles.

There are no disputes about Sophocles' authorship of the plays (as there are with Shakespeare), but a fascinating question remains: How could this man (who "suffered no troubles") have written such enduring literature?

The Story Behind the Story

All that we think of as Western drama from Broadway to high school productions evolved from ancient Greek drama, which itself had its own origins in even more ancient places. From the earliest times in all cultures some kind of play-acting—complete with fantastic masks and other disguises—has been part of the common life. These activities appear to have served some ritual purpose, but they did not constitute "drama" by the time it was flourishing in fifth-century Athens with productions by Aeschylus, Sophocles, and Euripides.

According to noted British scholar Alan H. Sommerstein in *Greek Drama and Dramatists* (2000), no one quite knows when or why these ritual play-acting events became unified performances with role-playing actors speaking from established scripts. A chronology included in the book shows that about 75 years before the birth of Aeschylus (earliest of the famous trio), a phenomenon known as "tragic choruses" became associated with the cult of Dionysus. These choruses sang lamentations for the misfortunes of public figures and later became an integral part of Greek tragedy.

Greek drama evolved into three genres: tragedy, satyr-drama, and comedy. The satyr-plays dramatized the clever and lustful antics of creatures with human, animal, and godlike features. Without human characters the plays stirred no deep emotions or asked no serious questions. Mainly, they provided bawdy entertainment that preceded the serious productions. Comedy is etymologically related to the rowdy songs of drunken revelers carousing up and down the streets. Comedy brought pleasure to its audiences by making fun of common human weaknesses and by exposing the schemes and impulses most people strive to keep hidden. Comedy's origins may have been political—an attempt by the participants to destabilize the ruling powers. According to Sommerstein, comedy served the political interests of both liberal and conservative factions. The standard fare of comedies included mistaken identities, happy resolutions of romantic relationships, and whimsy of all kinds.

Pomposity, greed, and hypocrisy were humorously treated without denying their serious consequences for human society; political satire was a mainstay. Catastrophes and deplorable fates for likeable characters were not permitted.

From the mid-third century onward, drama was a formal and distinct art form associated with the cultural greatness of the Greeks. Of the genres, tragedy was regarded as the most noble. Three plays by a single artist—performed as a set for official competitions—were viewed by as many as twenty thousand spectators (all or mostly male) seated in a grand, open-air, three-sided theater in the shadow of the Acropolis. The performance area was at the center and bottom of the theater with benches for spectators rising up and away. Platforms at different levels accommodated changes of scene and indicated the status of each character. A low wooden building behind the performance area had a central door for exits and entrances. Performances honored Dionysus—god of wine, revelry, and play-acting—and were linked to multi-day public celebrations that encompassed political and other cultural interests.

In contrast to comedy, tragedy took up the elevated issues of free will and fate, knowledge and illusion, and presented onstage the spectacle of noble human suffering. The technical features of these plays are so numerous that entire books are devoted to delineating them. Performers were male and wore masks to indicate age and gender, social standing, and sometimes, ethnicity. The main actors spoke in one of several variations of verse with all the features of poetic speech except rhyme: figurative language; alliteration; meter; and wordplay. A typical meter (syllable length and rhythm sequences) was iambic trimeter (x—u—x—u—x—u—, where 'u' is short, '—' is long, 'x' is either). Stage settings were not elaborate. Of the three major tragedians Sophocles was the most austere although he was known for using splendid costumes and music. Sophocles was responsible for some notable innovations: the introduction of a third speaking actor onstage (making for more complex interchanges); an increase in the number of chorus members; special focus on the central character; and development of the characteristics of the tragic hero. Greek scholar Bernard M. W. Knox writes definitively, "The unrelenting concentration on the central figure ... is the Sophoclean hallmark" (*The Heroic Temper*, p. 3). Sophocles also broke from tradition by producing plays that stood alone; he wrote no trilogies. The Theban plays—*Oedipus Rex, Antigone*, and *Oedipus at Colonus*—are frequently read as a unit because they overlap thematically and chronologically, but each has its distinct mood and integrity. *Antigone*, written first, belongs chronologically after *Oedipus Rex* and before *Oedipus at Colonus*. Each deals with different members of the same family at different periods of the family's life cycle. In Sophocles' rendering of the legend no family curse hangs over Oedipus and he is the main investigator of his own case.

The best-known traditional element of Greek tragedy is the chorus—the onstage performers of song and dance—which functions as a single voice or even a single idea in material form. In the absence of explicit stage directions, the alternating dialogues among protagonist, chorus, and the other actors divide the play into discrete sections; these provide the structure for Greek tragedy. Aristotle in his *Poetics* (c. 350 B.C.) named and defined these elements: the "parados" is sung as the chorus arrives at its section of the stage called the "orchestra"; the "stasimon" is performed while the chorus occupies the orchestra; the "prologue" occurs before the chorus makes its first appearance; the "episode" is the activity between the songs; and the "exodus" is the activity that follows the final choral song.

The chorus has multiple functions. The odes summarize the preceding action or speculate about its significance; both help clarify the issues for the audience. By anticipating the horrifying acts to come, the chorus can act as a kind of companion to the audience: a shock prepared for is a shock mitigated just enough to keep people in their seats. Generally the chorus stands (like the audience) outside the action, but (unlike the audience) makes comments and often has a stake in the outcome. The chorus also functions as a normative standard against which the protagonist struggles. Since the consequences of the action in tragedies are generally frightful, the chorus response can sound like the voice of humanity itself. By framing and elevating the ideas inherent in the action, the chorus is offering them to the audience for its own speculations. Finally, the chorus stands in opposition to the dreadful notion that the universe is without meaning. Its monumental task is to make sense of the suffering it has witnessed onstage, thus keeping order intact and chaos at bay.

Bernard Zimmerman in *Greek Tragedy: An Introduction* explains the different ways the tragic poets used the chorus:

> In Aeschylus [the chorus] serves as a vehicle of the dramatic action, and in Sophocles becomes a distinct dramatis persona with a minor part in that action. The Euripidean chorus, by contrast, dismayed at what is happening around and in part because of it, no longer participates in the action but only sympathizes with the actors. (24)

Greek tragedy has two conceptual components—the material itself and the ideas generated by the onstage action. Writers of tragedy took their material from legend and myth—sources that lent themselves to variations in the retelling. Homer, Sophocles, and Euripides all took up the Oedipus story, but differed in their treatment of Oedipus's blinding. In Sophocles, the blinding is self-inflicted and generates complex and varying interpretations; in Euripides, Laius's men inflict the blinding; and in Homer no blinding occurs. Playwrights could assume their audiences were familiar with the old legends; their task was to present the material in original ways.

The most prominent features of Greek tragedy are the spectacle and mystery of human suffering. The phenomenon of suffering—omnipresent and universal—stirs the intellect as well as the heart. The notion of a single figure of high prominence at the center of the tragic action originated with Aristotle in *Poetics*. He observed in the old tragedies a turning point ("peripeteia") that takes the protagonist from a position of power and success to a state of misery and misfortune—to being, as King Oedipus says of himself, a "zero." This figure came to be known as the "tragic hero." Aristotle also established the concept of the flaw or fatal lapse of judgment ("hamartia") that is said to bring about the "fall" of an otherwise masterful and virtuous personality, and the related idea that pity and terror are aroused in the spectators by witnessing the tragic action. Aristotle singled out *Oedipus Rex* as the purest example of Greek tragedy, but centuries of attention to all forms of tragedy has established the validity of more than one narrative pattern.

Aristotle is of course not alone in singling out the play for special praise. Prominent scholar of Greek tragedy Charles Segal notes that *Oedipus Rex* occupies the same position in literature as the *Mona Lisa* does in art (*Oedipus Tyrannus: Tragic Heroism and the Limits of Knowledge*, 2001, p. 3). And Freud brought a different kind of fame to the play when he used the Oedipal story in his *Interpretation of Dreams* (1900) as a paradigm for the unconscious desire for parricide and incest. The Oedipus complex has persisted as a major and widely recognized (also disputed) cultural concept.

Although the Oedipus plays have never fallen out of favor, *Oedipus Rex* didn't reach its full prominence until the late 18th and early 19th centuries when there was a shift in European intellectual circles away from the Latin masters (Seneca, etc.) to the Greeks (beginning with Homer). Intellectuals of the Romantic period were especially drawn to the profound questions about personal identity that the story of Oedipus raised. Earlier, the poet John Milton devoted himself to understanding Sophocles; the playwright's influence is seen in Milton's *Samson Agonistes* (1651). The first printed edition of Sophocles' plays was published in Venice in 1502. A chapter in Ruth Scodel's book provides an interesting history of how the plays were transmitted over the centuries. She points out how amazing it is that they survived in manuscript form for 1,900 years, and reminds her contemporary readers who have no trouble finding copies of the plays in any bookstore that such ready availability is relatively recent.

Performances of a play about parricide and incest could not be expected to avoid controversy and/or censorship. And, in fact, *Oedipus Rex* was caught up in the long and loud debate over censorship in the British theater. The play had been performed in its original Greek at Cambridge University in 1887, but professional productions were forbidden. In the *Cambridge Companion to Greek Tragedy*, Fiona Macintosh, Lecturer in English at the University of London, provides a detailed account of the production history of Greek tragedy during the 19th and 20th centuries. She reports that during this time a letter sent to Lord Chamberlain, a member of the Advisory Board on Stage Plays, advised against granting permission for performances of *Oedipus Rex* because it might "... lead to a great number of plays being written ... appealing to a vitiated public taste solely in the cause of indecency" (295, footnote 19). A license to perform was finally granted in 1910 by the Examiner of Plays.

Most Americans are familiar with this ancient play or at least recognize elements of the story. Scholars have numerous explanations for its widespread appeal. The plight of the tragic hero arouses a potent mix of feelings—attraction and revulsion, awe and horror, and Aristotle's fear and pity. With Socrates, we are caught up by the play's ambiguity and complex view of causality. The Roman philosopher Lucretius offered his famous explanation for the strange pleasure that comes with witnessing the enactment of tragic emotions: "Sweet it is, when on the great sea winds are troubling the waters, to behold from land another's deep distress ... to look upon armies battling on the plains without sharing in the danger" (Collins 22). Other readers have noted that human beings have been grappling for centuries with the fearful mystery of undeserved suffering that the play so memorably embodies. In our own time we cannot avoid coming face to face through the media with the grim spectacles of genocide, civil wars, torture, and the awesomely destructive powers of nature. All these involve the suffering of innocents on a grand scale. Finally, another reason for the play's appeal, scholars remind us, is its novel distinction as the first great detective story in Western literature.

Greek tragedy and the related concept of the tragic hero have acquired a special status in Western culture. While reading

Oedipus Rex it may prove interesting to keep in mind that a passionate (but unorganized) number of readers and scholars insist on the importance of protecting the original and "pure" definitions of these words in our language. It is commonplace, for example, to hear described as a "tragedy" an event that might more accurately be called a "calamity," a "disaster," possibly only a "mishap," maybe even a "catastrophe." The words are used interchangeably. Here is something to ponder: Is there a value to preserving a definition of tragedy that prevents its use in describing the entire range of personal or collective misfortune? Clearly there are differences between the sorry fate of a person fatally struck by lightning and the tribulation undergone by a figure like King Lear, Antigone, or Oedipus. It is possible that by knowing the character and circumstances of the person struck by lightning we might conclude that a genuinely tragic episode had occurred instead of a lamentable or catastrophic one. In general, concern about what constitutes "heroic" behavior or a "tragic" character is not high in the priorities of most people. But what if something inestimable and essential about human life is lost by allowing these categories to be blurred or diluted? The great playwright Arthur Miller made a case for seeing tragic dimensions in the life of what he called "the common man." Willy Loman in *Death of a Salesman* (1949) was his example. *Oedipus Rex* brings the reader face to face with this issue. Readers may decide that their experience with the play is, among other things, an opportunity to reflect on whether these issues matter for the individual or cultural life.

List of Characters

King Oedipus appears in myths older than the plays of Sophocles. His name connects him to his origins and character. Abandoned as an infant on a mountainside, with his ankles pierced to ensure his death, Oedipus later walks as an adult with swollen feet—one of the meanings of the words that make up his name. The circumstances of his birth, lineage, and life have made the art of knowing and the consequences of not knowing (the Greek *oida*, "I know") the essential task of his life. Oedipus has two personalities in the play; or more accurately, he reveals two sides of his complex character as the play unfolds. In the beginning he is a model of Athenian virtue; he is masterful, optimistic, confident, and benign. When his reign is threatened he becomes suspicious, wrathful, punitive, and tyrannical. His fall from royal status and happy matrimony to shameful banishment has become the symbol of the reversal of fortune. Oedipus's relentless and self-ruining pursuit of truth is the mark of a noble mind; his gesture of self-blinding is an unforgettable compensatory act of humility.

Jocasta is sister of Creon, widow of Laius, and doomed wife and mother of Oedipus. Jocasta's robust and authoritative intervention in the argument between Creon and Oedipus displays a concern both maternal and queenly for the stability of family and kingdom. Jocasta unwittingly sets in motion the unraveling of the mystery of Oedipus's identity by providing information meant to have the opposite effect. Her bold and irreverent question about the reliability of oracles raises the issues—central to the play—of fate and free will, the role of Chance in the events transpiring, and the nature of divine justice. Later she exposes her ambivalence about the gods by making an offering to Apollo. After realizing the truth of the terrible prophecy and failing to prevent Oedipus from his own discovery of it, Jocasta flees to their bedroom and hangs herself.

Creon is brother to Jocasta and brother-in-law to Oedipus. The chaotic Sphinx and her nefarious riddle sabotaged his brief reign as king of Thebes following the death of Laius. The name *Creon*, from the Greek *kreon*, means "ruler" or "king." Is it strange—or a sign of Sophocles' perceptiveness—that the king's brother-in-law who makes a famous declaration against wishing to be king bears this name? Creon's protestations of innocence against Oedipus's accusations of treason are not fully convincing. At the end of the play Creon does replace Oedipus as king of Thebes, but he shows no signs of gloating or excessive pride. In *Antigone* Creon's character changes; his rule of Thebes is rigid and authoritarian.

Teiresias was a legendary Theban seer with supernatural gifts of clairvoyance and prophecy. The goddess Minerva bestowed these gifts on Teiresias to compensate for his loss of eyesight. He was said to have both male and female characteristics to enhance his ability to know all that was, is, and will be. Teiresias is given a prominent role in T. S. Eliot's *The Waste Land*. In *Oedipus Rex* Teiresias is as reluctant to tell what he knows as Oedipus is eager to hear it. The arrival of the seer effects a change in Oedipus from being a benign king concerned for his people to a ruler indignantly defending his royal status. Teiresias lives by intuition and symbol; Oedipus by power and directness. The clash between these two giant figures contributes to the dramatic energy of the play.

The **Chorus** is distinct from the supplicants. It is drawn from a representative group of educated and reflective citizens, although it speaks with one voice. The chorus is loyal to Oedipus and resists any accusation made against him without proof. Witnessing the unraveling of the chorus's faith in its king is one of the painful experiences of the play. When the validity of oracles is questioned, the chorus experiences great anxiety. It sings its famous ode about the consequences of losing belief in a divine order. One of the functions the chorus has is to anticipate and deflect the rising terror felt onstage by the other participants, including the audience. When terror can be held at a distance, the chorus takes up another of its functions: it analyzes what has happened and then speculates about meaning and consequences.

The crowd of **Suppliants** that approaches Oedipus represents the diverse population of Thebes currently suffering the afflictions of the plague. An elder calling himself the **Priest** of Zeus addresses Oedipus reverently and beseeches him to find the cause of the plague and a way to end it.

The **Servant** of Laius is summoned by Oedipus to tell his version of the murder at the crossroads. He holds the key to Oedipus's guilt or innocence. Oedipus says he killed all the men, leaving no survivors; the servant claims to have been the sole survivor. If the servant's story is true, Oedipus was not implicated in that event and is not guilty of being the murderer of Laius. This servant turns out to have been the one Jocasta referred to as "the other hands" charged with carrying out the terrible act of abandonment, the individual who, in an act of mercy, saved the child and gave him to the shepherd of Polybus and Merope.

There are two **Messengers**. The first arrives at the palace to announce the death from old age of Polybus, father of Oedipus and king of Corinth, and the related news that Oedipus will be called as the new king. The news provides Oedipus and Jocasta a brief respite from the anxiety they have experienced, fearing the oracle's prophecy that Oedipus would be the cause of his father's death. Their relief is short-lived. The messenger goes on to identify himself as the shepherd who was given the infant Oedipus and who in turn gave him to the childless king and queen. In this way Oedipus learns a critical piece of his own riddle—that he is not blood-related to Laius. The second messenger brings the news of Jocasta's suicide.

Antigone and **Ismene** are the daughters of Oedipus and Jocasta. Their brief appearance at the end of the play to say good-bye to their blinded and ruined father adds to the enormity of the horror onstage. They come at the invitation of Creon, who, in this gesture, reveals a measure of generosity and respect for the fallen Oedipus.

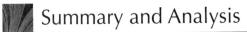

Summary and Analysis

1.

Audiences and readers have had several centuries to ponder Sophocles' *Oedipus Rex* and come to conclusions about its meaning and effectiveness as a play. Despite all this time and attention, there is still no consensus about the play. It is simply too dense with issues both timeless and timely. More than one hundred years ago, Clifton W. Collins, while acknowledging the complexity of the play, pointed out another marvel: the deceptively simple plot. "An oracle foretells that Oedipus shall slay his father and marry his mother; and, against his own will and knowledge, he fulfills his destiny" (Collins 20). This description is not quite accurate. The separate enactments of parricide and incest have occurred or been initiated offstage; graphic renderings of horrible deeds were rarely depicted onstage in Greek drama. What the play does provide is a retelling of the life of Oedipus from fortuitous rescue on the deserted mountainside to celebrated kingship to precipitous fall—all compressed into a matter of minutes on the stage. As classics scholar Ruth Scodel writes: "... the play is the unraveling of its own prehistory" (58). The action is fast paced. There is no protection from the shocking conclusion, no interesting distractions along the way, and no escape from the devastating impact of Sophocles' dramatic irony.

An inquisitive spirit—a compulsion to ask questions—permeates the play. Oedipus's first utterance is a question: "Children ... why [are you] here with your suppliant crowns?" His question sets in motion a series of increasingly self-incriminating answers that in turn generate more questions throughout the play. Essentially all questions are variations of the one that comes to mind when one is looking down at one's feet on the earth and up at the stars in the edgeless universe: Who am I and what am I doing here? These questions become matters of life and death for Oedipus. The play's dramatization of these and other fundamental questions is one reason for its wide-ranging power and appeal. One way for the new reader to frame the question is to focus on the issue of responsibility. It is the one that generates the most passionate disputes and comes in many variations. Did the gods preordain the fate for Oedipus that Apollo prophesied or did Apollo foresee Oedipus's fate and direct him to discovering it? Did Oedipus invite his own fate through some error or flaw? Is divine justice ever comprehensible from a human perspective? These matters of free will and predestination, of choice and determinism, and of responsibility and accountability are always relevant and engaging. After grappling with these timeless issues, the reader may decide to focus on the more manageable questions about how the play works as a play. In either case the main activity on- and offstage is one of discovery.

The terms used here to mark divisions in the play come from the twelfth chapter of Aristotle's *Poetics*. The songs and dances performed by the chorus are essential for defining these divisions. The prologue is the part of the play that comes before the chorus makes its first appearance. The *parados* ("entrance from the side") is the song presented by the chorus as it moves onstage. The *stasimon* ("standing song") is the song the chorus sings from the orchestra, its place on the stage. "Episode" refers to the sections of the play occurring between the songs and "exodus" to all that follows the final choral song. Strophe ("the turn") is the first major stanza in a choral ode and antistrophe ("counterturn") follows; they are metrically identical. Sometimes the alternating strophe and antistrophe function as a mind in debate with itself.

In the chronology of the Oedipus legend, *Oedipus Rex* tells the first part of the story. In the opening scene before the assembly of beleaguered supplicants, Oedipus radiates the essence of royal power and dignity. He is masterful, confident, compassionate, prescient, and ready to act in the service of his subjects. It is the job of the king (or president or prime minister) to keep chaos at bay in his realm, and Oedipus, in word and demeanor, conveys confidently and unhesitatingly his intention to do so. Moreover, he has connected his own interests with those of the larger group, establishing unity within Thebes with his words: "My spirit groans for the city and myself and you at once". He addresses his people like a father to his children. Thebes is like an extended family.

The plague is not present in every version of the Oedipus story. It is Sophocles' innovation to link the two, and he may have been inspired by a real plague that had recently ravaged Athens (430 B.C.) after the city became flooded with refugees from the Peloponnesian War. The plague afflicting Thebes is more than a spreading of infectious agents (such as typhus, the likely historical scenario). As described by the priest whom Oedipus calls upon to speak, this plague behaves like a preternatural event—an assault on the regenerative sources of life itself: women of childbearing age, seeds, and female cattle. The Greeks believed that destructive acts of nature were the work of the gods; the prospect of sterility—the end of life on earth—would therefore suggest that a monumental offense violating the order of creation had been committed. The dread that overhangs Thebes is akin to that in *Hamlet*: "Something is rotten in the state of Denmark." And in that play as well, incest and the murder of a family member are involved.

In his study of the poetry in Sophocles' work Herbert Musurillo points out the powerful imagery in these early lines of the play. In addition to vivid scenes of blighted landscape, there is the priest's reference to Thebes as a ship "... reeling like a wreck ... scarcely [able to] lift its prow out of the bloody surf." Musurillo writes, "[Thebes] is wallowing in blood, in death, as the bodies fall in the city and empty the state of its manpower [and] the ship of its crew" (83). Later in the play Jocasta refers to Oedipus as the "pilot" of their communal ship. This ship-of-state imagery continues and intensifies in the play. Later Teiresias will warn Oedipus: "[no] harbor shall there ... be for your cries." Thebes, once a saved and safe harbor for Oedipus, will become a paradox—a "harborless harbor." Such imagery would have special meaning for the Athenians who had always to be vigilant against invasions from the sea.

The Theban citizens have staged a kind of demonstration in front of the palace, and their very presence poses a question to Oedipus about what he can do to save them. They regard their king not as godlike but as their esteemed leader who has pitted his intellectual power against the abominable Sphinx and won. In their view the "pestilence and plague ... some furious god [is hurling on the city] bloating Hades [with bodies]" will find in their king a formidable foe.

The legendary confrontation between Oedipus and the Sphinx is not enacted in the play, but every audience in Sophocles' time knew the myth and would have understood the reference. The figure of the Sphinx—a lion's body with a human head—is more ancient in origin than Greek tragedy. The Sphinx made its first appearance as a symbol in the age of the Fourth Dynasty (c. 2400 B.C.). In Greek mythology the figure is female and equipped with wings. Perhaps the addition of wings was made to expand the range of its destructive powers. The noted English scholar of Sophoclean drama, R. C. Jebb, describes the Sphinx succinctly and memorably as a "manifestation, in mind and body, of a force with which mortals may not cope" (227).

The devastation inflicted on Thebes by this remorseless and intractable figure disrupted Creon's reign as king following the murder of Laius. The Sphinx demanded an answer to her infamous riddle and dashed to bits the body of each poor soul who tried and failed. The people are in desperate need to put order against chaos, and Oedipus's fame for solving the riddle and dispatching the Sphinx was well deserved. The riddle asked for a definition: what being is it that sometimes has four feet, sometimes two, and sometimes three; speaks with a single voice; and is weakest when it has the most. Phrasing her riddle deceptively, the Sphinx tricks her victims into thinking only an exotic answer will work. The answer is quite simple, however, and Oedipus gets it at once. He addresses the Sphinx:

Man is it thou hast described, who, when on earth he
appeareth, first as a babe from the womb, four-footed
creeps on his way, then when old age cometh on,
and the burden of years weighs full heavy, bending
his shoulders and neck, as a third foot useth his staff.

To the man who could accomplish this feat, the despairing Creon had offered the throne and his widowed sister as wife.

Oedipus had just arrived at the stricken city after deciding to leave his home in Corinth to escape the fate foretold him by the oracle at Delphi. Thus he had come to be both savior of Thebes and famed solver of riddles. He assumed the throne and went on to marry Jocasta. They had two sons, Polynices and Etocles, and two daughters, Antigone and Ismene. Under his reign Thebes enjoyed a peaceful interlude and Oedipus enjoyed prosperity and wedded life. This brief reference to the happier circumstances in the life of Thebes and its king will have the effect later in the play of making Oedipus' fall more precipitous and shocking, and much harder to witness. The story of Oedipus's life is so old that audiences everywhere knew (and know) the outcome before the play begins. The challenge Sophocles faced in having to present the familiar material in arresting ways is accomplished in the image he creates here of Oedipus towering graciously and masterfully over his people with no inkling of the doom the audience knows awaits him. Created at the start of the play, this dual narrative is responsible for much of the dramatic tension and pleasure in the play. In this opening scene Oedipus is enjoying what he will soon remember as his final moments of unqualified public acclaim. His people have come seeking another dramatic rescue. In keeping with his proactive character, Oedipus has already sent Creon to seek advice at Delphi.

2.

The shrine at Delphi honoring Apollo has already delivered two important oracles for the story (neither is enacted in this play). The first was the oracle that informed King Laius that his own son (not yet born) would murder him and then wed his wife. The second was the occasion much later when Oedipus consulted the oracle about his true identity (after it was called into question by a countryman). He was told that he was destined to kill his father and marry his mother, but—unhelpfully—not who they were. Creon's visit is the third. The Greeks looked upon this shrine as the most sacred spot in their country, occupying the place Jerusalem would come to have for Christians. Apollo—one of the "sky gods" who lived on Mount

Olympus—was associated with many skills and qualities, among them: light, sickness and healing, music, archery, and prophecy. Over his temple were inscribed the words "Know thyself"—a fitting injunction for a play about self-discovery.

In making Creon his emissary to the shrine, Oedipus has made two critical and revealing choices. He has initiated the act of problem solving he is already known for, which in turn will lead to the tenacious pursuit of truth he will become known for. The appropriate humility he displays in deferring to the god Apollo for guidance represents simultaneously a retreat from the self-reliance that served him so well with the Sphinx. And while his decision to send Creon shows a willingness to entrust others with important affairs of state—an admirable component of enlightened leadership—Oedipus has also empowered his brother-in-law and one-time king to be the first to hear, and then interpret, the divine message for the entire kingdom. Is this sharing of power a reckless gesture or a sign of some deep uneasiness about oracles? Oedipus has already received one disturbing message from the oracle; perhaps it isn't strange that he has no wish to hear another. No clarities about Oedipus's motivations are given for these complex decisions. This may be Sophocles' insight and it makes sense to us: even to ourselves our own motivations are enigmatic.

Bearing sprigs of laurel—a hopeful sign for the expectant citizens—Creon makes a stately return and announces that a remedy for ending the plague is at hand: "a pollution grown within the land [must be driven] out." Pressed by Oedipus for details, Creon relates for all to hear again the story of Laius's murder that the oracle has linked to the city's pollution. It is unlikely that Oedipus would be ignorant of the momentous event that elevated him to his reign of Thebes and marriage to Jocasta—and all the elders would be expected to know as well—but, dramatically, this retelling by Creon serves to inform the younger supplicants and to restate for the audience some important details.

Creon has fulfilled his responsibility to Oedipus, but there are some puzzling aspects about his way of doing so. It has taken him more time than seems necessary to deliver an urgent message with such important consequences. He doesn't directly answer Oedipus's directly posed questions. Instead Creon makes an ambiguous statement: "[The answer is] a good one. Even what is hard to bear, I say, may end up in good fortune if it comes out right." Creon's evasiveness is unmistakable. He does not say, "The oracle says ..."; he says, "I say...." He is interpreting the answer not reporting it, and Oedipus must now publicly confess to feeling apprehensive. He goes on to ask twelve more questions before the scene ends. In effect, Creon has maneuvered Oedipus away from a position of power and into one of vulnerability. As professor and classics scholar Frederick Ahl observes in *Sophocles' Oedipus: Evidence and Self-Conviction*, "... Creon speaks as enigmatically as an oracle, thereby becoming an oracle Oedipus must consult.... Instead of asking what the oracle actually said, Oedipus asks whether Creon's words mean he should hope or fear" (57). What is Sophocles attempting to expose here about Creon?

The few lines remaining before the chorus arrives contain several examples of Sophocles' famous irony. Already Oedipus has boldly declared that "[he] ... may prove a villain, if [he does] not do all the God demands." But he is already the villain. Then he says the grief he bears is actually more for his people than for himself, although we know this will not be true in the way he intends. He also encourages Creon to make the prophetic message public—a gesture of admirable openness on the king's part, but also one that will seal his fate: once the words are public there will be no way to keep these disclosures hidden—and possibly avoided. But Oedipus's virtue is that he is not a devious or fearful ruler. He also has no conscious inkling yet of his own complicity. To Creon's account of the murder and the oracle's identification of the murderer's presence in Thebes as the cause of the plague, Oedipus says he knew Laius only "by hearsay" but "[had never] seen him." To prepare for the discovery and capture of the villain, Oedipus asks pointed questions about the robbery and murder. Creon describes a band of murderers, but Oedipus in almost every subsequent reference uses the singular "robber": "How could a robber dare a deed like this were he not helped with money from the city, money and treachery?" Does this preoccupation with one rather than several robbers expose Oedipus's anxious premonition about his own culpability? In his mind must remain prominently the memory of a recent fatal confrontation of his own. This series of questions marks a shift in Oedipus's attitude—from unwavering concern for the Theban people to anxiety about his own status and future. He will now "act in [his] own interest," he says, "[because] whoever he was that killed the king may readily wish to dispatch me with his murderous hand; so helping the dead king I help myself." Until Oedipus learns that he is the cause of his kingdom's suffering, these utterances, especially those that display his virtuous and likeable qualities, are profoundly and painfully ironic for the audience that knows about the anguish awaiting him.

It is difficult—even at this early point in the play—to hold all these ironies in mind at the same time. For example, we will shortly learn more about the decision Oedipus made to leave Corinth. It was precipitated by doubts about his own identity that a remark by a random Corinthian had forced him to confront. He journeyed to the shrine for information and heard for the first time the oracle's prophecy that he would slay his father and marry his mother. To escape this dreaded and dreadful fate, he decides to leave Corinth, assuming his parents to be the ones he is leaving behind. A critical point to remember about this decision to escape his fate by leaving Corinth is that it is precisely this sojourn that brings him directly and unwittingly to his fatal encounter with Laius and then to his arrival at Thebes to outwit the Sphinx and become its new king. If a fate has been decreed by the higher powers, is there ever a way to escape it? The unintended consequence of his decision to escape his fate was to become the king of Thebes, and, as king, to become its beloved healer and its new disease, its savior and its new curse. Sophocles' Oedipus is more than complex; he is a paradox; one could say a kind of riddle himself.

3.

After addressing the crowd of supplicants, Oedipus withdraws to his palace. The citizens hopefully disperse and the chorus of elders arrives to begin deliberations to save the kingdom. The singing of the parados—the traditional entry song—announces the arrival of the chorus, its several members speaking throughout as one voice. The chorus stands on its own, distinct from the suppliants and not partial to any political faction. Later in the play Jocasta calls them the "lords of the land." Sophoclean scholarship has established that the chorus is not the voice of the playwright. It is reflective and well informed and functions like a group of well-respected consultants that considers possibilities and consequences. The plague fills the chorus with "terror and trembling," and tortures its collective mind like one "stretched [on] a rack of doubt." In recounting the "numberless miseries" endured by the Theban people the chorus adds a grim detail: even the dead remain infectious and continue to spread disease.

The chorus stands ready to join forces with Oedipus. Its traditional opening prayer calls for deliverance and healing through the agency of three deities, identified as the "three averters of fate": Athena, patron goddess of Athens, famous for her wisdom; Artemis, twin sister of Apollo and upholder of the earth; and Apollo, giver of prophecy. The chorus links the plague with warfare and specifically solicits divine aid against the war god Ares. Scholars are puzzled by this detail, because war is not associated with Thebes during the mythical reign of Oedipus. Some have suggested that in the interest of grounding his plays in real and contemporary events, Sophocles may have been making use of the Athenian engagement in the Peloponnesian wars that were ongoing during his lifetime.

Oedipus returns to the stage and addresses the chorus as an equal. Throughout this scene the exchanges between them are impressively open and democratic. Oedipus seeks advice from the chorus and entrusts it with some of the responsibility for rescuing and restoring the kingdom. The authoritative tone of his words conveys an appropriate and familiar confidence, but his choice of words suggests a subtle shift of emphasis. In his brief absence from the stage, he appears to have decided to put a slight distance between the common fate and his own individual fate. Where he was once quick to reassure the citizens of his personal identification with their plight, he now refers to himself as a "stranger to the story [and] to the deed" and as one who although a citizen now was not always a citizen. Nonetheless Oedipus restates his great loyalty to Thebes and declares his determination to be its savior for the second time. His proposal is less severe than he might have made it: whoever comes forward confessing to the murder of Laius will suffer exile but not harm or death. He is more punitive toward the one who is found out and also to anyone who shields the culprit. "Hear what I should do then," he announces, and proceeds unwittingly to call down upon his own head the unthinkable curse: a complete severing of all ties to kingdom, family, and religious observance—in effect, a separation from the source of love, meaning, and hope, from life itself. Then follows this dreadful and dreadfully ironic warning: "... whether he is one man and all unknown, / or one of many—may he wear out his life/ in misery to miserable doom! / If with my knowledge he lives at my hearth / I pray that I myself may feel my curse." This long speech of Oedipus brings new ironies. Before it ends he has declared his commitment to defending ("[as if] for [his] own father") the house of Laius, while lamenting the unfortunate demise of its family lineage. After announcing its own innocence of the murder, the chorus urges Oedipus to follow the advice of Apollo's oracle and seek out the name with the help of the clairvoyant Teiresias. Once again true to his character, Oedipus has been proactive and already sent for the famous seer. With the reassurance of mutual respect between king and his compatriots and a re-stating of their overlapping commitment to the common good, the scene comes to a close.

The chorus calls Teiresias one "... in whom alone of mankind truth is native." This remark is more than a statement of high regard. For the Greeks, the dividing line between humans and gods was the ability to foresee the future. Teiresias is unique among men; even after his own death, he continues to prophesy. A sign of his special insight is his own physical sightlessness; a little boy leads him onto the stage. In his welcoming greeting, Oedipus conveys a deep reverence for Teiresias, speaking as a king to another of similar royal stature.

Teiresias's opening words are curious. Is he addressing himself or Oedipus when he declares, "Alas, how terrible is wisdom when / it brings no profit to the man that's wise!"? Both possibilities make sense: for reasons known only to him wise Teiresias doesn't want to be there; wise Oedipus will soon be undone by his earlier display of wit. Surprisingly missing from Teiresias's initial statements are expressions of concern for the welfare of Thebes, or even acknowledgment of its suffering. He has been summoned to aid the collective effort but he seems focused on Oedipus alone. Oedipus is understandably impatient, even indignant, at this early point over what seems to him an inexplicable and inexcusable disregard on the part of Teiresias for the city that has nurtured him. Stunned but still hopeful, Oedipus makes a gesture only the truly great are capable of: he proposes that "all of us," himself explicitly included, become supplicants and kneel in humbleness before Teiresias. Teiresias speaks enigmatically, but his rejection of Oedipus's request is clear and resolute: "I will tell you nothing." This refusal to be of service is rare for a seer (although it was not regarded as a crime) and it raises some questions not answered by the play. Was Teiresias showing magnanimity by not wishing to reveal something he knows will ruin Oedipus? Would his silence have saved Oedipus from his fate? Or is his declared reluctance to speak part of a strategy designed to arouse Oedipus's (and everyone's) curiosity and so build a momentum toward the revelations he later makes? Whatever the explanation, this unexpected response first prompts disbelief and then offense. Fully provoked now, Oedipus enters into a heated exchange with Teiresias who proves to be equal to the challenge. From a state of disbelief Oedipus moves quickly to one of alarm: he accuses Teiresias of plotting the murder of Laius and—in defiance of the order Oedipus himself has just issued—of protecting the one or ones who carried it out. In some translations, Oedipus accuses Teiresias of "fathering" the plot to kill Laius, a choice of word that suggests the unconscious anxiety he has reason to be experiencing. Teiresias, insulted and now also fully provoked, yells the terrible truth back at Oedipus: "You are the land's pollution."

The exchange between these two giant figures demonstrates a clash between different kinds of power and different ways of knowing. Oedipus is direct, impatient, and overt. His power inheres in his royal status, and he deals with what is apparent and urgent. Teiresias is reticent and indirect; his strength comes from perceiving truths that are not apparent. Oedipus for example has entirely missed the import of Teiresias's allusion to the king's temper:

Oedipus
> You would provoke a stone! Tell us, you villain,
> tell us, and do not stand there quietly
> unmoved and balking at the issue.

Teiresias
> You blame my temper but you do not see
> your own that lives within you; it is me
> you chide.

Oedipus
> Who would not feel his temper rise
> at words like these with which you shame our city?

Teiresias is thinking of "temper" as something other than a momentary outburst; he is pointing to an underlying pattern in Oedipus of being quick to judge and quick to act. This observation about Oedipus is the first clue offered in the play about an element in his character that may contribute to his fate. And, in Oedipus's accusation of Teiresias, we have just witnessed an instance of hasty and irrational judgment; he has no evidence to support it. So why does he make his accusation so forcefully? Is paranoia a component of his character that simply has had no occasion to be drawn out before now? Or is Oedipus using the accusation to disguise a judicious retreat to strategy: if he maligns the integrity and motivation of Teiresias, others will be less inclined to believe his assertion that Oedipus is the city's pollution. Again, no clarity about Oedipus's own motivations is given, but the puzzling range of possibilities makes him a complex figure and his fate less easy to comprehend. A compelling feature many readers of Sophocles' plays report experiencing is a call to make judgments about the guilt or innocence of the characters, the rightness or wrongness of the positions and attitudes they hold. And the characters themselves are so compelling that we are drawn into their stories and want to make sense of their actions and fates. Yet we never have enough knowledge to do so. This masterful scene is an example of Sophocles' power to engage his audience. Witnessing the verbal and psychological duel between king and seer must have mesmerized early audiences.

When Oedipus succeeds in provoking the reluctant Teiresias to speak again, he and the assembled citizens, who are by now listening in rapt attention, hear a more explicit and shocking accusation: King Oedipus is the murderer of Laius and an egregious sinner living in the foulest dishonor with those most beloved to him. The rage that erupts in Oedipus at Teiresias' words disables his capacity for seeing and thinking clearly. Seeming to forget that his welcoming remarks to Teiresias included praise of the seer's special vision, Oedipus turns on the old man and ridicules his physical blindness. Moving now from alarm to paranoia, Oedipus declares his innocence and his determination to prove it by insisting that Creon is joined in conspiracy with Teiresias against him. No evidence is produced for this pronouncement as none is for the accusations of Teiresias, but Teiresias stands firm while Oedipus rages on.

On top of the conspiracy theory he has leveled at Teiresias, Oedipus adds a reminder of his own formidable skill with the Sphinx, hoping that one or the other will suffice to resecure his rule of Thebes and the trust of the people. Sounding like Jehovah in the Old Testament Book of Job admonishing humankind to remember its puny state in the universe, Oedipus imperiously chides Teiresias for failing to solve the riddle with his useless "knowledge got from birds" while he, "know-nothing Oedipus," using his unassisted wits saved Thebes. This magnificent speech—Oedipus reminding his kingdom of his wisdom and devotion—contains another of the dreadful ironies of his life, this time embedded in the misplaced sarcasm of "know-nothing." "Your life is one long night so that you cannot / hurt me or any other who sees the light," says Oedipus to Teiresias—words that will soon come to describe his own life. Oedipus ends this exchange by darkly hinting that were Teiresias not old and blind, his alleged treason might be punished by physical torture. In this scene—a matter of some minutes onstage—Oedipus has moved from making regal declarations of reverence and solicitude to hurling wild and wrathful accusations, even threats of torture. In the presence of Teiresias, Oedipus has undergone a total change of personality: from the one seeking investigation to the one being investigated; from the solver of a life-and-death riddle to a riddle unto himself and the solution to a life-and-death riddle for his kingdom.

Felix Budelmann provides a different perspective on this transformation in his book *The Language of Sophocles*. Budelmann traces the incremental changes in Oedipus's perspective, beginning with the opening scene when the king identifies his own interests with those of the kingdom. In dispatching Creon and summoning Teiresias, Oedipus has acted as if there "is only one communal wish: that the *polis* be saved" (207). Budelmann uses the Greek word *polis*, which refers to "the citizen body" with its implication of the common good. The words "city," "town," and "Thebes" bear a similar meaning. Budelmann points to Oedipus's earlier remark about the perceived threat to his own life from the killer of Laius as the first instance in the play where the king diverges from serving the common good and toward his own survival. But the moment passes quickly, and until the exchanges with Teiresias, Oedipus is primarily focused on ending the plague and restoring health to all citizens. By the conclusion of the scene with Teiresias, Oedipus has come to see himself as standing proud and alone, defending his rule, his attention diverted from the plight of the city. The plague has almost been forgotten! The chorus, which has been looking on, steps forward to help redirect the focus back to unity and the discovery of "God's [best] meaning for us." The effort fails; the chorus is ignored and both men carry on as if it had not spoken. "Thebes, and its survival, is no longer the unrivaled centre of attention" (Budelmann 219).

Teiresias begins the first part of his final speech with an odd remark: he claims his right to speak in his own defense as if a tryannical Oedipus had taken it away from him. The implied accusation is false; Oedipus made it clear he was seeking answers from all corners and specifically asked Teiresias to speak and had to beg him to do so. What might this erroneous statement tell us about Teiresias? Perhaps in those first ambiguous opening lines that lament "how terrible is wisdom when / it brings no profit to the man that's wise!" Teiresias was exposing his jealousy over Oedipus's success in solving the riddle. Whatever Teiresias intended to imply in those lines, his comments have the effect of undermining both his trustworthiness and his appeal, even though, as the audience knows, his prophecy will prove to be true. He goes on to deliver more prophetic words that highlight the central theme and imagery of the play: the manifold levels and meanings of "seeing." "You have your eyes but see not where you are / in sin, nor where you live, nor whom you live with," Teiresias tells Oedipus, then asks, "Do you know who your parents are?" This amounts to a much scarier existential question: Does Oedipus know who *he himself* is? Oedipus is so alarmed by now that he hasn't been able to listen. "What parents? Stop! Who are they of all the world?" he asks a few lines later. This inattentiveness is entirely credible. Oedipus has just heard his terrible fate from Teiresias that blinded and bereft, he will be driven from his kingdom; his ship-of-state will have no harbor; and—the greatest humiliation—he knows nothing.

Teiresias has the last words and again they are puzzling: "I have said what I came here to say...." But earlier he insisted he had come intending and wishing to say nothing. Teiresias is nearly as enigmatic as Oedipus. He leaves Oedipus with an image of himself as a lonely sojourner in a foreign land, "tapping his way before him with a stick." Whereas Teiresias, "[the] seer of truth," cannot be violated—"there is no way you can hurt me," he informs Oedipus—Oedipus will become by way of prophecy a doomed and paradoxical figure. Not only both son and husband to Jocasta and father and brother to his children, Oedipus has been turned into the answer to the Sphinx's riddle: a man in his third phase of life, old and weak now, walking with three legs, one of them a cane. It would be difficult to imagine a more ironic outcome. Solving the riddle brought him fame, power, and love. Enjoying these successes brings ruin down upon him. Frederick Ahl writes about these ironies: "[Teiresias] has used his rhetorical skill to refute Oedipus as utterly as Oedipus had refuted the Sphinx. Indeed, Teiresias has made Oedipus the new Sphinx plaguing Thebes. And he, like the Sphinx of Old, will be destroyed by words" (102). In the scenes that follow, Oedipus himself will bring forward the evidence that leads to the end of his reign and subsequent banishment.

4.

The separate departures of Oedipus and Teiresias from the stage make space for the chorus to respond to what it has just overheard. The dilemma facing Thebes has taken a dramatic turn. The urgent question of what to do about the plague has been upstaged by the more urgent question about the murderer's identity and whereabouts: "Who is the man proclaimed / by Delphi's prophetic rock / as the bloody handed murderer, / the doer of deeds that none dare name?" It is no wonder that the chorus goes on to describe its state of mind so memorably as being "in a flutter of foreboding."

The image the chorus has of the villain as a wild bull lurking in the mountains, a sad outcast with "lonely feet" is surely ironic for the audience that knows the actual villain has moments ago been standing next to the chorus, requesting its help. Reference to the "lonely … feet / that carry [the murderer] far from the navel of earth" brings to mind the meaning of Oedipus's name. The Greek *oida* meaning "I know" or "I have seen" is appropriate for one who solves a great riddle but does not know his own identity and ends up unable to see. "Oedipus" also has roots in words meaning "swollen feet" which link him to his origins as an abandoned child, to his subsequent lameness, to the feet in the Sphinx's riddle, and to the image we have of him at the end of the play, blinded and walking barefoot in exile.

In its dislike of the uncertainty facing the city, the chorus commences its duty of considering different explanations for what has befallen its kingdom, hoping to find a reassuring resolution. Lacking evidence supporting the view that Oedipus would have had reason to kill Laius, the chorus must withdraw its complete faith in Teiresias and conclude that although he is a revered and trusted seer, he is also merely human and must have made a faulty prophecy. Drawing on its memory of Oedipus's valor with the Sphinx, the chorus concludes with a statement of loyalty to the king—"till I should see the word / proved right beyond doubt."

Creon appears before the chorus to express dismay and indignation about Oedipus's accusations, and even to question the king's sanity. "Were his eyes straight in his head?" asks Creon. Wishing to downplay the seriousness of these charges and countercharges, the chorus offers the possibility that Oedipus was influenced by a passing "gust of anger." Its efforts are cut short by Oedipus himself who arrives exhaling his own indignation at Creon for daring to appear before the palace.

Their ensuing dialogue reveals important differences between the men. Creon speaks in low and reasonable-sounding tones. "… When I know nothing, I / usually hold my tongue," he says, a pointed remark that effectively contrasts himself to the immoderate Oedipus. Making use of the Sophist's method of persuasion, in vogue during Sophocles' lifetime, Creon artfully composes his protestations of innocence. First, he draws from Oedipus an acknowledgment that he, along with Jocasta, shares power with Oedipus and occupies a priviledged status in the kingdom. Then, posing as a man of virtue and moderation, he asks why anyone in his privileged position would want to be king with its full burden of responsibility and "troubled sleep."

It is true: in contrast to Creon, Oedipus is a raving man. And it is also true that he has made hasty, irrational, and erroneous accusations against Creon and Teiresias, and had the audacity to do so with no compelling evidence. High temper and impatience do indeed undermine reasonableness and tempered responses. In Oedipus's case, they even seem to have eclipsed the original and overriding concern for the general welfare in order to make room for concentrating on retaining his own power. We will learn later in the play that just these same personality features displayed here by Oedipus—high temper and impatience—also influenced the outcome of his fateful encounter with Laius at the crossroads. This scene is not the end of the play, however. We will see an evolution in Oedipus that takes him beyond his madness and self-absorption, and that may put the characters of Teiresias and Creon in a different light. For now it is worth remembering that Creon's name comes from the Greek word *kreon*, meaning "ruler" or "king." In an earlier scene we witnessed Creon assuming a position of power over Oedipus in his manner of relaying Apollo's message. In this scene Creon has taken the liberty to address the chorus as if it were his ally alone. And by questioning the sanity of the king before the chorus, Creon was perhaps deliberately seeking to disparage Oedipus in its eyes. Like Oedipus and Teiresias, Creon is a complex figure and much of his motivation remains hidden, even to himself. By the end of the play, he will have become the king he insists he does not wish to be. His kingly manner, however, is neither gloating nor unkind.

The chorus intervenes again to diffuse the tension rising between Creon and Oedipus. It urges Oedipus to restore calm by believing the sincerity of Creon's words, but in vain: Oedipus exposes more of his self-concern by countering Creon's remark about the king having lost his wits with an admission that "... for [his] own interests [he] has [his] wits about [him]," and the conflict escalates when Creon claims a share of the city's future as his right. "In the nick of time," the chorus is relieved to announce, Queen Jocasta arrives onstage.

Jocasta delivers a powerful opening speech. She confronts these two contentious and all-powerful men and orders them off the stage:

For shame! Why have you raised this foolish squabbling
brawl? Are you not ashamed to air your private
griefs when the country's sick? Go in, you, Oedipus,
and you, too, Creon, into the house. Don't magnify
your nothing troubles.

Jocasta's presence brings a traditional female influence into
this all-male world: her first instinct is to quell the fractious
voices and restore order. She then redirects the attention
to the original and overwhelming problem—the communal
suffering—and chides the two men for neglecting it. Their
"nothing troubles" are dismissed as childish squabbles. Jocasta
has the right priorities but not the right facts. She is unaware
of the accusation and prophecy Teiresias has delivered, and she
has no reason to suspect her own complicity.

Creon addresses Jocasta as if they are allies—with Oedipus
the outsider. Then Oedipus appeals to her loyalties, certain they
will stir her to come to his immediate defense. Whatever power-
sharing had been arranged among these three, and which Creon
was referring to earlier, has evaporated in this brief exchange.
Creon puts himself under oath to make his declaration of
innocence more formidable and it works; Jocasta is persuaded. The
chorus joins in, urging Oedipus: "Be gracious, be merciful...."

Up to and including this scene, the chorus has used
common sense and the obvious need for unity to make its
points. Referring to Creon's alleged treason as an "obscure
conjecture" of Oedipus's mind, the chorus may have been
intending to alleviate the king's paranoia, but appears to have
only exacerbated it. The exchange that follows is bewilderng.
Oedipus seems to have lost all equanimity and all magnanimity.
He equates his willingness to consent to the chorus's pleas to
spare Creon with the chorus's wish for his death or banishment.
This dreadful assumption moves the chorus from "a flutter of
foreboding" to a "broken spirit" brought on by the anguish
of passionately divided loyalties: it loves Oedipus and Thebes
equally and sees no clear way to resolution. This pained
outburst by the chorus—"May I die without God's blessing
... if I had any such thought [of wishing Oedipus dead or

banished]"—shows the fuller range of emotions it is called upon by the artist to represent at critical moments.

Oedipus relents; he bows (but not graciously) to public and private pressure (the chorus and his wife). His decision, which saves the kingdom from having to endure another ordeal, appears to be a gesture of realignment with the larger community. He does not, however, explain his motives for releasing Creon nor does he show any evidence that he understands them himself. The long series of questions he has just put to Creon about Thebes at the time of Laius's murder did not quiet his suspicions of treason. When he asked about Teiresias's role—"At that time did he say a word about me?"—Creon replies evasively, "Never, at least when I was with him." The question is legitimate: if Oedipus was indeed the slayer of Laius why didn't Teiresias share his special knowledge of it then? In these exchanges Creon has made a show of reasonableness but not of credibility, or not full credibility, while Oedipus has failed to prove a conspiracy or establish his innocence. In the manner and content of these exchanges, Sophocles has left both chorus and audience with the question of who is telling the truth.

And why does Oedipus let this irresolution stand? It is one of the mysteries of the play. Perhaps he is not thinking clearly, as Creon repeatedly points out. But we can imagine that in such circumstances even the most self-possessed king might not be able to hold everything together in his mind. What clearly does emerge in the action is Oedipus's tyrannical nature. "I must be ruler!" he declares, exposing an important internal shift in attitude: Thebes must be saved so he can rule it.

Creon exits the stage but not before he mockingly accuses Oedipus of sulking "in [his] yielding." Such a remark—made by a man who has just been spared death or banishment—sounds unnecessary, mean spirited, and provocative. It does, however, contain an apt and prescient observation about what he calls Oedipus's "dangerous" temper: "… natures like yours / are justly heaviest for themselves to bear." Creon's exit leaves Jocasta, Oedipus, and the chorus on the stage. When he returns, he will do so as the new king of Thebes.

5.

In the moment of relative calm that descends after Creon's departure, Jocasta asks to know what has just happened. Her request displays a reasonable and apparently harmless curiosity, but it unintentionally sets in motion the rapid unraveling of the mystery and the undoing of her union and reign with Oedipus. The chorus, anticipating the consequences, instructs Jocasta not to get involved. This is not the first effort in the play to obstruct the discovery of truth. Teiresias made the first one by determining not to speak. And, as with Teiresias, this effort also fails. The instinct the chorus has to spare both Jocasta and the community from experiencing the pain that comes of knowing too much is no match for Oedipus's inquisitive nature. After alienating Teiresias and Creon, Oedipus then alienates his most loyal ally—the chorus—by ignoring its concerns and acquiescing to his wife's request: "Yes I will tell you. / I honour you more than I honour them."

Oedipus's dismissal of the chorus is callous and hasty. It also reflects the transformation we have seen taking place within him. Were he still the great king of Thebes of the opening scene, he would have detected the "broken spirit" of the chorus and regathered its members into his circle of protection and compassion. He would, in other words, have reinstated the priorities of the land and resumed his effort to find the murderer of Laius. But by now his self-concern has all but eclipsed his concern for everyone else in Thebes. Frederick Ahl makes this additional observation:

> Oedipus does not grasp that people have individual motives for their actions: professional prestige for Teiresias, power for Creon, protection from the powerful for the chorus. His egocentric paranoia translates disparate motives into conspiracy, his tyranny empowers him to act willfully. His willfulness allows others to assimilate him to the negative, tyrannical paradigm, yet his own self-doubts make him an indecisive tyrant. With or without a conspiracy, then, the outcome is the same: a coup d'etat. (130)

It is important to remember the changes in character that Oedipus undergoes in these scenes because—later in the play—we will be unable to avoid grappling with the justice or injustice of his fate and we will need to understand as fully as possible who he is. For the same reason it is also important to observe about Oedipus that however hard he is working in these scenes to establish his innocence he is also surrendering to an inward and apparently unstoppable determination to find out the truth. His nature is split by two conflicting and all-powerful instincts: to save Thebes and to save himself. He is a man profoundly divided against himself. We witness this self-ruining drive being enacted in the way he relentlessly extracts damning information from Jocasta.

Jocasta is curiously both innocent and wily in these exchanges. After listening to Oedipus's not quite truthful account of Creon's alleged conspiracy with Teiresias against him and the seer's prophecy of his guilt, she launches into a vigorous and startling speech asserting that oracles can be false and seers fallible. The obvious intention of her words is to reassure her husband that his fears are groundless, but they have the additional effect of successfully diverting her husband's attention away from her brother's alleged complicity. Like the other major actors in the play, Jocasta has a complex mix of motives and desires.

Jocasta's words have the opposite of their intended effect. The story she uses to illustrate the falsity of oracles is one she thinks she knows well: the prophecy Laius received that he would be slain by his own son. To reinforce her point, she recounts the story of Laius's murder at the crossroads not by the hand of a son but by a band of robbers. The story creates spasms of anxiety in Oedipus instead of calm. He cannot stop himself from asking questions. Each detail he elicits from Jocasta deepens his sense of doom until he is seized by fears of a different and far more daunting kind of conspiracy: "What have you designed, O Zeus, to do with me?"

According to Jocasta's story, the murder of Laius and the crowning of Oedipus happened in the same time period. These and other details are sufficient evidence for Oedipus to place himself and Laius on the same road at the same time each heading in the direction of the other. He will soon disclose to his wife his fatal encounter with a traveling group on the road. He must now consider that the group was that of Laius and his entourage and that he could be the murderer of the king.

The unraveling continues. Jocasta goes on to describe Laius's strategy to escape his prophesied fate: he ordered that his three-day-old infant son be abandoned on an inhospitable mountainside, and, in the unlikely event that the child survived starvation and exposure, his feet were to be "pierced" (in some translations, "yoked") making rescue an even more remote possibility.

This speech is striking for several reasons. The first is its improbability. How much of this information would Oedipus—now married to Jocasta for many years—not know? Dramatically the speech makes perfect sense. It provides critical details for the larger narrative and it accelerates the rising anxiety within Oedipus even as it draws out the time he must wait before arriving at the truth. Also striking are the extreme measures Laius took (and Jocasta permitted) to escape his fate. (For contemporary audiences such measures are unimaginable as well as criminal, but for Athenian audiences in Sophocles' time rather more commonplace.) Finally, the self-assured tone Jocasta uses to reassure Oedipus seems incautious, especially for speculations about such fundamentally unknowable questions.

> So Apollo
> failed to fulfill his oracle to the son,
> that he should kill his father, and to Laius
> also proved false in that the thing he feared,
> death at his son's hands never came to pass.
> So clear in this case were the oracles,
> so clear and false. Give them no heed; I say....

Athenian audiences—if not contemporary ones—would not have failed to detect the hubris reflected in her speech.

Oedipus's response is to ask still more fateful questions, this time about Laius's physical appearance. When Jocasta answers—"in his [appearance] not unlike you"—Oedipus feels the weight of truth descend upon him: "O God, I think I have called curses on myself in ignorance…. I have a deadly fear that the old seer had eyes." Oedipus has no reason yet to suspect he is the son of Laius; he appears to recognize no conscious link between the pierced feet of the infant and his own flawed feet. The "deadly fear" he speaks of must therefore come from the reinforcement of his suspicion that the man he killed was indeed the former king. A lesser man might choose to ask no more questions, but it is in the nature of Oedipus—as his name makes clear—to want to know and to want to see. And there is still the possibility of his innocence that more questions could establish.

"Foreign highway robbers" are identified as the murderers. Oedipus knows he acted alone. If the man said to be the lone survivor of the attack can be summoned to tell his tale, and his report about more than one assailant remains unchanged, Oedipus will know himself to be innocent. According to Jocasta, the survivor, a servant she calls "an honest man" begged to be sent off as far away as possible from Thebes after learning that Oedipus had replaced Laius as king. An explanation for the servant's bizarre behavior is not given, but "an honest man" he was not able to be at the time. The surviving servant was—improbably—also the servant who helped save the infant Oedipus. He knew all the details of Oedipus's origins and rescue and did not want to witness the enactment of their dreadful consequences.

The failure of her efforts to reassure Oedipus bewilders Jocasta, and she uses her "worthy" standing to demand an explanation. Like one who has been harboring intolerable secrets and finally given a chance to release them, Oedipus launches into a long recitation about his own life. Again the speech is literally improbable. Would Jocasta actually need to be told the names of her husband's parents and who they were? But again, dramatically, the speech is essential—not only for the new details but for its psychological power. Oedipus is caught up in a terrifying ordeal: the slow transformation before his eyes of illusion into truth, of appearance into reality. The illusion is his own self, his identity as he has known it all his life. The truth is the identity others are pressing upon him and the awareness emerging within him at the same time. At this depth of insecurity one is drawn to one's origins; Oedipus begins by identifying his parents and moves quickly to the detail that will turn everything on its head: the accusation of illegitimacy made by some random and inebriated citizen.

A seeker even then, Oedipus does not let his parents' reasurrences stand until he discovers the truth for himself. The charge of illegitimacy ("this thing," he calls it) "rankled always." Like his actual father before him, Oedipus seeks Apollo's advice through the oracle and learns about the "desperate horrors to befall [him]," the very parricide and incest that plague his kingdom. Also like his father, Oedipus moves quickly to escape the prophesied fate. These are the ironies for which Sophocles is famous: precisely the effort Oedipus makes to escape his fate is the one that brings him face to face with it. The futility of trying to escape fate is a commonplace belief in Greek tragedy. The more vexing questions are about guilt, responsibility, and how to conceptualize fate. Is fate a force acting from above and beyond with no relationship to its victim? Is it predetermined by character? Is it simpler or more complex than either of these conjectures? The play appears to be an intentional dramatization of these questions.

Oedipus, in relating his story to Jocasta, realizes he may have called down upon himself the dreadful curse he ordained for the murderer of Laius. But he dreads even more a fate far worse: that however unintentional and unknowing his actions were, he is the one responsible for them, for the unspeakable acts of parricide and incest that violate all laws of nature and of the gods. Here is his cry:

O no, no, no—O holy majesty
of God on high, may I not see that day!
May I begone out of men's sight before
I see the deadly taint of this disaster
come upon me.

The chorus—which by now has all but forgotton the plague—counsels Oedipus to keep his hope alive until he hears the servant-now-shepherd's story. But once alone on the stage following the departure of Oedipus and Jocasta, the chorus is more free to speak its mind. To release the escalating tensions it has been absorbing from holding back its worst fears, the chorus delivers its famous ode about hubris and tyranny and the potential for the collapse of all meaning and order. It begins by restating its own belief in "the laws that live on high ... begotton in the clean air of heaven [in which] God is great ... and grows not old." Without speaking of Oedipus by name, the chorus attacks pride and excessive ambition and warns against their consequences. Ever reasonable, the chorus at the same time acknowledges that some measure of ambition is useful: "[May] God ... never abolish the eager ambition that profits the state."

The chorus represents the thinking elders and citizens of Thebes. For it to have to confront the possibility that oracles might be neither true nor reliable is equivalent to questioning its own reason for being. "Why," the chorus asks itself and the audience, "if a man [who] walks with haughtiness ... and gives no heed to justice and [despises] the shrines of Gods ... reaps gains without justice and will not hold from impiety.... Why should I honor the Gods in the dance?" More simply stated, why should the chorus perform the religious function assigned to it if the whole world of belief that it represents is meaningless? More simply still, why pray if no god listens? Why follow the laws if they are capricious or baseless?

The chorus has just been confronted by the possible unreliability of Teiresias, in whom it had placed its highest trust. Now, confronting the possibility that the gods themselves are unreliable, the chorus declares it will "[no] longer to the holy place ... go to worship ... unless the oracles are proved to be fit, for all men's hands to point at." The chorus experiences despair about this prospect and profoundly wishes for the restoration of oracles as authentic messages from the gods without, ironically, any inkling of what this would mean personally and for the kingdom. It ends by praying to Zeus to ensure the credibility of oracles in the future.

This choral ode has drawn comment from many readers. In her book focused entirely on the Sophoclean chorus, Cynthia P. Gardiner discusses this and other ironies in the ode. She points out that the audience has enough information to know that the chorus's wishes will be fulfilled by the end of the play:

> Somehow it will be shown that oracles will become reliable again because they were never false and that the gods will bring down *Hybris*—not merely the voluntary kind that the chorus fear, but an involuntary kind that they have never imagined. The irony is particularly ingenious and terrible because it results from the general principles of religious belief, rather than mere personal joy, which the chorus espouse in all ignorance but which the audience then applies to the specific circumstances, so as to react with horror. (105)

She makes another important point about the way the timing and placement of the ode contribute to the dramatic tension necessary at this point because the audience knows what to expect when the news of the death of Polybus is delivered:

> The poet must prevent the slackening of tension and the sense of anticlimax that would naturally accompany an action which the audience has been expecting; unless, of course, he deliberately fosters the audience's expectations in order to cheat them.... It would be repetitious here for the chorus to speculate on the facts: Did Oedipus kill Laius?.... If they were, on the other hand, to condemn him or Jocasta for foolishly scoffing at oracles, the audience would simply nod in agreement and continue, perhaps with fading interest, to expect the obvious. Sophocles has therefore given the chorus a song whose ironies will generate such a feeling of horror, and pity for the chorus, that it must engage the audience's full attention and participation. (Gardiner 106)

The Greek scholar E. R. Dodds points out that in the ancient world religion and prophecy were linked. By giving this speech to the chorus, Sophocles may be speaking to his Athenian compatriots. In his essay, "On Misunderstanding the *Oedipus Rex*," Dodds imagines Sophocles asking:

If Athens loses faith in religion, if the views of the Enlightenment [promoted by the Sophists] prevail, what significance is there in tragic drama, which exists as part of the service of the gods? (*Twentieth Century Views of "Oedipus Rex,"* 27)

But the chorus does dance. It has been deeply shaken but it acts to reaffirm its belief or to keep despair at bay; both are possible. It also tends to another of its functions in the play, namely, to consider the far-ranging consequences of the action taken up on the stage. In effect, the chorus has been warning against the danger for the body politic if oracles are regarded as untrustworthy: human order would collapse and anarchy prevail.

Dodds takes this occasion in his commentary to raise the question of divine justice, a question that becomes all-consuming at the end of the play when the audience witnesses the suffering Oedipus must endure. Dodds reminds his readers that the Greek view is not the Christian view:

To the Christian it is a necessary part of piety to believe that God is just. And so it was to Plato and to the Stoics. But the older world saw no such necessity. If you doubt this [read] the *Iliad* ... or ... the Book of Job. Disbelief in divine justice as measured by human yardsticks can perfectly well be associated with deep religious feeling. 'Men,' said Heraclitus, 'find some things unjust, other things just; but in the eyes of God all things are beautiful and good and just.' [Heraclitis, fragm. 102] I think that Sophocles would have agreed. For him ... there is an objective world-order which man must respect, but which he cannot hope to fully understand. (27–28)

Jocasta returns to the stage in a changed mood. A new air of urgency suggests something has transpired between her and Oedipus while they were alone inside the palace. She is carrying flowers and incense, a sign that she is seeking protection from the gods she has dismissed moments earlier as irrelevant. She now seems frightened by Oedipus's behavior, even implying, as Creon before her, that he is insane, and conveys the seriousness with which Oedipus regards the dire predictions. In the accelerating panic she seems to include herself now. "The pilot of our ship," she calls Oedipus, recalling the earlier image of Thebes as a ship floundering at sea. Frederick Ahl points out that in no other scene in Sophocles does the Greek word for fear (*phobou*) appear so densely. In the one hundred or so lines between Jocasta's agitated return to the stage and the conversation Oedipus has with the Corinthian just before he learns his true parentage, "fear" is used nine times. "This episode is, then, the episode of fear in a tragedy of fear" (Ahl 156).

6.

The arrival of the man from Corinth bearing his message about the death of Oedipus's father, Polybus, is the beginning of the end of the plot's disentanglement—the moment Aristotle named the *peripeteia*, the reversal of fortune moment. Interesting to note here is that even for this nameless person, Sophocles has given introductory remarks dense with ironies: "Might I learn from you, sirs, where is the house of Oedipus? Or best of all, if you know, where is the king himself?" The ironies would have been more accessible to the original Greek-speaking audiences, but they are worth noticing even for contemporary audiences who appreciate Sophocles' subtle wit. In *Oedipus at Thebes* Bernard Knox translates these lines with transliterated phrases to make this point:

Strangers, from you might I *learn where (mathOI' hoPou)*
is the palace of the *Tyrannos OIDiPOUS,*
best of all, where he himself is, if you *know where (katOIsth' oPOU).*

"These [are] violent puns," writes Knox, "suggesting a fantastic conjugation of the verb 'to know where' formed from the name of the hero who, as Teiresias told him, does not know where he is" (63). Ahl comments on Knox's observations:

OIDa in Greek means "I know," and *POU* means "where." The echo of the syllable *POU* at the end of each of the messenger's first three lines emphasizes a play on OIDiPOUs' name. And how fascinating it is that the Corinthian should be the one to produce it here as he enters; for he will convince Oedipus not only that he knows *where* Oedipus comes from but that he can interpret Oedipus' name on the basis of another etymology: that of *OIDA*, "swollen," and *POUS*, "foot," which appears here for the first time in surviving Greek literature. (Ahl 157)

Oedipus and Jocasta leap to the good news that the death of Polybus did not come by his son's hand. Although this outburst of hope will be short-lived, it generates some bizarre behavior and interesting speculations. Jocasta shows herself to be capricious in her loyalties. Oedipus's father dead of presumed old age? Jocasta who just made homage to the gods now exults: "O oracles of the Gods, where are you now?" Oedipus seems to have fallen into hysteria ("Ha! Ha!.... [These oracles are] dead as he [Polybus] himself is, and worthless.") This unseemly outburst can be understood as coming from a sudden release of anxiety. But what are we to think of his strangely unfeeling reaction to his father's death. No reason has been given to suggest that any father/son animosity existed between Oedipus and Polybus. Oedipus especially, but Jocasta too, appear to suffer from a deficit of normal feeling.

Also interesting is the possibility that oracles might be interpreted figuratively. Oedipus suggests that Polybus may have "died of longing for [his son]" as an alternative to a physical slaying. And Jocasta offers her famous observation that caught Freud's attention and may be said to have set in motion the psychoanalytic movement: "As to your mother's marriage bed,—don't fear it. Before this, in dreams too, as well as oracles, many a man has lain with his own mother." This is the Oedipus complex: the son happy to have his father dead and fearfully free to imagine sexual union with his mother.

This Corinthian fellow is an anomaly. He presents himself as a messenger but is evasive about identifying his origins or allegiance. And his motivation for bringing the "good news" appears to be hope of receiving some reward once Oedipus returns to Corinth as the newly crowned king (the "good news" that Jocasta ignores and Oedipus never hears). Oddly, Oedipus pays him special attention, confessing his ongoing preoccupation: "I fear the living" (his mother, Merope, the other half of the prophecy). Whatever motivation (or carelessness) Oedipus has for exposing his vulnerability to a random visitor, it is through this vulnerabilty that he, the once-invincible ruler of Thebes, invites the penultimate piece of damning revelation: he, a foundling, is not the true son of Polybus, because the Corinthian, identifying himself now as the savior of Oedipus, rescued Oedipus from exposure and unfettered his feet. This means as well that Merope is not his true mother. To the ears of Oedipus this news means that the prophecy may still be true. To the ears of the Corinthian this news is a means of manipulating Oedipus into returning to Corinth: no longer must he fear his Corinthian parents; he must instead flee from his actual parents, whoever they are. Ahl writes, "The self-seeking Corinthian and the inquisitive Oedipus are moving down different pathways to their tragic intersection" (173). This same Corinthian, this random and apparently insignificant bearer of significant information, also speaks a line of perfect and succinct insight. To Oedipus, who is explaining the fear that's kept him away from Corinth, he says: "Son, it's very plain you don't know what you're doing." Is this remark a sign of Sophocles' sense of humor or an expression of egalitarianism?

Hope—short-lived and foolish—balances the fear in this scene, but cannot endure against the gravity of what has transpired: the acts of parricide and incest that violate the natural order. The smaller instances of futile hope—Oedipus in the survivor's report, Oedipus and Jocasta in the Corinthian's message about Polybus, and Oedipus in the Corinthian servant who was charged with the task of abandoning the infant—stand against the pervasive hopelessness of the play's narrative. Bernard Zimmermann in *Greek Tragedy: An Introduction* writes interestingly about hope:

> "Hope" (elpis), so fatal to human understanding, is a key word in the play. Used from the beginning ... in the context of Oedipus's search for Laius's murderer, its significance becomes even more evident when the chorus, in its entrance song, elevates the idea to the status of a divinity ... on a par with the Olympian gods. It was hope that led Laius to have his newborn son exposed in the mountains to thwart Apollo's oracle and avoid being killed by his own son; it was hope that led Oedipus to believe that by never again setting foot in Corinth he could avert the fate that had been prophesied to him by the Delphic god. (76)

Of the consequences of false hope, he writes:

> ... the farther Oedipus progresses in his search for Laius's murderer at the prompting of the third oracle, the closer he comes to the truth of the first two oracles and the deeper he penetrates into the past. And the closer he comes to what he imagines to be the truth and salvation, the closer he comes to the abyss of self-knowledge. (76)

Jocasta is the first to put all the pieces together, the first to solve the second riddle of Oedipus's life, and the first to absorb its gravity. Just moments after she has boldly declared that chance rules the world—"Why should man fear since chance is all in all for him?"—and advised against caution and reverence—"Best to live lightly, as one can, unthinkingly"—Jocasta listens silently as the messenger describes finding the infant on the slopes of Mt. Cithaeron, his feet pierced just as Laius had ordered. And Jocasta must also hear the messenger take responsibility for having given her son and husband his name. "Oedipus," for "swollen feet"; it is the affliction Oedipus has endured for a lifetime and the simple clue to the Sphinx's cryptic riddle: Oedipus the infant on all fours cruelly wounded so he could not escape; Oedipus the mature man standing tall, two-legged, ruler of Thebes; and Oedipus, the lame and blinded man, wandering into exile, relying on a cane.

From this point on, Jocasta acts, as Teiresias did earlier and as the old shepherd will in the next scene, to withhold information from her husband, even, to obstruct his effort to find it—an act equivalent to attacking his very nature that compels him toward full discovery of the truth. "O Oedipus, God help you! God keep you from the knowledge of who you are!" she cries. Each character here is intractably caught in a situation with no adequate or right response. This is catastrophically true of Jocasta. The next time we hear her name it is uttered by the distraught servant who rushes from the palace to announce her suicide.

But Oedipus is not to be deterred, not even by his beloved wife. To her urgings against seeking knowledge, he takes the opposite view: "I could not possibly be persuaded not to hear the truth." If Oedipus is driven by a will to power, he is clearly even more powerfully driven by a will to know the truth. This strangely moving observation about Oedipus has redemptive powers.

The lines Oedipus speaks are translated by Bernard Knox and discussed by him in *The Heroic Temper*. Knox is interested in delineating the features of the Sophoclean tragic hero: among them, his intransigence and imperviousness to the views of others, and his inflexibility and unwillingness to compromise. Knox sees these traits in Oedipus and refers to them as the hero's inability to yield. He writes:

This is the appeal made to all the Sophoclean heroes. To yield, to give ground, to retreat.... What do you want me to concede to you?" ... says Oedipus *tyrannos* to the chorus, when they implore him to reconsider his death sentence on Creon. It so happens he does make this concession, but in such a way that Creon tells him, "You are hateful in your yielding".... The hero refuses to yield. And in his demand that he should, he uses another word characteristic of the Sophoclean tragic situation, 'to *leave* alone, allow, let.' "Leave me alone, get out"...shouts Oedipus *tyrannos* to Creon, and later, a broken man but still of the same heroic temper, he says to Creon, "Leave me to live on the mountains." (16–17)

Jocasta, the chorus, and Creon—those who are caught up in the maelstrom of the hero's emotions—have only their reason and common sense to offer him. Jocasta insists that pursuing the messenger's story "will be wasted effort"; the chorus advises reasonably to spare Creon's life, and Creon explicitly uses reason to argue against any motive he might have for wanting to take the throne away from Oedipus. In response, as Knox observes, the hero takes leave of his senses, as Oedipus does when he misinterprets his wife's ominous flight from the stage as her indignation at the discovery of his alleged "low birth." To the chorus's frenzied warning that "... trouble will break out of this silence [the queen's absence]," Oedipus rants: "Break out what will! ... I account myself a child of Fortune, beneficent Fortune, and I shall not be dishonoured." The energy in his voice is daemonic and elemental. And so powerful it briefly pulls the usually self-composed chorus into the delusion. The chorus suggests that Oedipus has meta-natural origins, born of a "long-lived nymph who lay with Pan," more than mortal, and less. Oedipus too appears to regard himself as beyond the ordinary, as "kinsman to the months," allied with time itself: this is surely hubris.

7.

This mania comes to an abrupt end with the arrival of the old shepherd who received the infant from Laius and chose not to let him die and who was also the only survivor of Oedipus's fatal retaliation against Laius and his men. The bearer of the final revelation is at hand, but like Jocasta and Teiresias before him, he is determined to keep knowledge from Oedipus. Even at this last moment Oedipus could choose to escape the truth and keep his kingdom. But he is relentless, presiding over the scene as prosecutor, defendant, and jury with one goal: to know the truth. Sophocles makes this final scene of discovery long and almost unbearably tense; Oedipus must drag the truth out of the unwilling shepherd to bring to light the truth that will bring his own ruin: he *is* the son of Laius; prophecy is restored; and the gods continue their reign.

But there is another view of these events. Some scholars point to the possibility of an alternative interpretation that takes note of the several inconsistencies in the messengers' reports and the unknowable intentions motivating Creon and Teiresias. The prevailing view is that what happens onstage is an accurate accounting of that period of Theban history although there are perfect reasons for Sophocles to have intended otherwise: the play is, as E. R. Dodds writes, "about the blindness of man and the desperate insecurity of the human condition" (26). Readers interested in this line of inquiry will find Frederick Ahl's book helpful. Ahl writes:

> Here … is the essence of Oedipus's tragedy. He will not believe Polybus and Merope when they name him as their child, but he will believe an anonymous drunk at a party, an anonymous Corinthian who is seeking to line his own pockets. He will even believe, on secondhand testimony, that he has killed Laius, despite the fact that his own memory of a similar killing differs in several important details. And we readers draw the same conclusions on the flimsy grounds. Sophocles' great achievement here is to make us believe what Oedipus does: to disregard or rationalize away everything that might demonstrate the hero's innocence. (207)

About Teiresias, Ahl comments, "Teiresias is a professional seer, surpassed in mantic skills only once, in the riddle of the Sphinx, by Oedipus. In this play he may well take his revenge" (207).

Oedipus calls himself thrice accursed: in his birth, in his marriage, in his killing. The imagery of the state as embattled ship at sea is revisited here in the chorus's reference to the "great harbor" Oedipus has been residing in and the "furrows plowed by father and son": graphic images of his sexual and filial violations. Teiresias' warning of the "harborless harbor [for] his cries" also comes to mind.

The chorus reacts with horrified pity to the plight of their king and enlarges its circle of compassion and frame of reference by including with "luckless Oedipus" all the "generations of men" who must endure the illusory foundations of mortality: "Oedipus, you are my pattern of this. Oedipus, you and your fate!" Oedipus becomes here emblematic of all mankind.

Why does Oedipus blind himself?

The messenger's gruesome report and the unforgettable scene of the blinded king himself staggering from the palace back onto the stage is so abhorrent and heart-stopping that it is impossible at first to grasp onto any meaning at all. Teiresias knew this was coming. He made riddles for Oedipus about insightful blindness (his own) and blind sight (Oedipus's). Oedipus has been a proud and confident ruler. Recalling these riddles would put him beside himself: the insight larger than his capacity at that moment to absorb it. Teiresias was right; Oedipus's own eyes have deceived him. This dreadful realization has been coming on in waves; when it crashes over Oedipus, the rash act he makes of tearing out his own eyes is a savage punishment, but strangely understandable.

Bernard Knox tells us that a single Greek word describes the action and character of all tragic heroes; it means "strange, dreadful, terrible" (*The Heroic Temper* 23). E. R. Dodds reminds us that "… in a sense everyman must grope in the dark as Oedipus gropes, not knowing who he is or what he has to suffer; we all live in a world of appearance which hides us from who-knows-what dreadful reality" (28). Oedipus's first response to the final revelation of himself as one "whom God … hates above all men on earth" is to beg the sun to disappear from his sight: "Light of the sun, let me look upon you no more after today!" The messenger reported that as Oedipus was tearing the brooches from his wife's robe and turning them into weapons against himself, he was "... shrieking out such things as: they [his eyes] will never see the crime I have committed or had done upon me!" In the brief moments it would have taken the blinded Oedipus to reach the astonished chorus he has added to his understanding. He tells the chorus that his act was freely willed; it came by his own hand and then: "Why should I see whose vision showed me nothing sweet to see?... What can I see to love?" Later he tells them another reason for his act:

I do not know with what eyes I could look
upon my father when I die and go
under the earth, nor yet my wretched mother—
those two to whom I have done things deserving
worse punishment than hanging. Would the sight
of children, bred as mine are, gladden me?
... [and] with what eyes shall I look upon my people?

Oedipus has been broken apart from himself, from everything he knew and everything he loved. Even his own voice doesn't seem attached to him: "Where is my voice borne on the wind to and fro?"

What guilt does Oedipus bear that brings on such suffering? For contemporary audiences Oedipus's acts of parricide and incest would not be crimes of the first degree because he committed them unwittingly. His intentions were good; the acts themselves evil. E. R. Dodds writes, "If Oedipus had been tried by an Athenian court he would have been acquitted—of murdering his father. But no human court could acquit him of pollution, for pollution inhered in the act itself, irrespective of motive. Of that burden Thebes could not acquit Oedipus, and least of all could its bearer acquit himself" (24).

The messenger's description of Jocasta's flight to her bedroom and her desperate crying out to Laius suggests that it is the horror of incest that drives her to take her life. Incest is more destructive of life than parricide; a single incestuous act violates the sanctity of both maternal and conjugal love. Of both acts, Christopher Rocco writes:

> In breaking the taboos against patricide and incest, Oedipus destroys the boundaries that separate the civilized city from savage nature, humanity from bestiality. By killing his father and wedding his mother, Oedipus disrupts the "natural" succession of generations. (43)

Rarely in Greek drama, as mentioned before, are acts on this scale of brutality enacted onstage. The effects are enough to fill any theater, and more. The chorus responds to Oedipus's self-blinding as anyone would: they think it is an act of madness—"What evil spirit leaped upon your life … a leap beyond man's strength!"—and don't want to look at him. The repulsion displayed here by the chorus is similar to the repulsion generated by acts of incest and parricide. Still, the chorus is humane, even compassionate. "Is he in any ease from pain?" it asks the messenger. Oedipus's response is similarly moving. Recognizing that the loyalty shown him by the chorus was genuine, Oedipus speaks these powerful lines:

> My friend,
> you are the only one steadfast, the only one that attends
>   on me;
> you still stay nursing the blind man.
> Your care is not unnoticed. I can know
> your voice, although this darkness is my world.

The final scene and lines have generated hundreds of pages of commentary, some of it memorably personal. Peter Meineck and Paul Woodruff, contemporary Greek and theater scholars, offer a new translation of the Theban plays and much erudite as well as personal commentary on them. Meineck recalls his first reading of the play as a young student, followed by many later readings. In *Sophocles: Theban Plays* he ponders: "… how could I have been fascinated by this play, when I knew from the first page that every moment brought the hero closer to a miserable discovery?" (xxxv). No matter how many times Meineck has read the play, he reports that he "[is] still unsure how to explain

[its] power" and remarks that even though we all know by the end of the play that "there is nothing left to happen but [Oedipus's] inevitable departure from Thebes…. [S]till, that long final quarter of the play is riveting" (xxxv). The scene with his daughters Antigone and Ismene, made possible by Creon's unexpected and unnecessary graciousness, is among the most memorable in the play.

An essay by Bernard Knox in *Twentieth Century Interpretations of "Oedipus Rex"* (1968) is devoted entirely to the final scene. Knox observes and discusses many of the qualities of Oedipus that make him more than a miserable man, make him, rather, a formidable human being and the embodiment of the tragic hero. In the last scene Oedipus restores to himself his own strongest qualities. An aspect of his greatness now is his capacity to renew his compassion for his city—although not in a way he could have imagined. He no longer represents the kingdom of Thebes (Creon must order him into the palace because kin are now his only appropriate company), but he can still think about its welfare from his humbled position. He tells Creon, "… never let this my father's city have me living a dweller in it." But something of his imperial self remains; he forgets that he cannot design his own fate—in this case, death, which he prefers—or exile. Creon has to remind him that he is in charge now and will consult the oracle before making a decision.

Oedipus's self-blinding can be understood in this context as a bold and imperial act and at the same time as a gift of compensation. The act against himself is as comparable to his violations against God and nature as any a single human being could devise. Jocasta's suicide is her gesture. Oedipus's gesture is an effort to be realigned with the order of the universe. In *The Heroic Paradox*, Cedric H. Whitman writes:

> [Oedipus] cannot ignore the crimes he has discovered he has committed; he must do something, and he chooses to sacrifice his eyesight. "Apollo destroyed me," he cries, "but I struck this blow" … meaning that his self-blinding is a freely offered token of the moral integrity he wills in contrast to the circumstances that have ruined him. (62–63)

Oedipus even maintains a kind of hope. Although he has—characteristically—been impatient and hasty when asking for his own death, he accepts exile and for once can speak truthfully about what he *does* know:

This much I know:
no sickness and no other thing will kill me,
I would not have been saved from death if not
for some strange evil fate. Well, let my fate
go where it will.

What a courageous thing to say! Oedipus is still willing to face everything. Knox writes, "He feels himself as eminent in disaster as he once was in prosperity ... whatever his end will be, it will be out of the ordinary, like everything else about him" (93). Oedipus, who earlier referred to himself with false mockery as "know-nothing Oedipus" and presumptuously claimed to know the dark truth about Teiresias and Creon's motives, can now say to the chorus with the confidence borne of transfiguring experience:

Approach and deign to touch me
For all my wretchedness, and do not fear.
No man but I can bear my evil doom.

In "Why Does Tragedy Please?," an essay included in *Tragedy: Vision and Form*, D. D. Raphael speculates about the "peculiar satisfaction" experienced by readers of tragic drama. "[It] comes from a feeling that the sublimity of the hero's spirit is superior to the power which overwhelms him. The dramatist stirs in us more admiration for the human spirit than awe for the powers of necessity.... [Tragedy] snatches a spiritual victory out of a natural defeat...." (196). And Edith Hamilton in her classic book, *The Greek Way to Western Civilization* (1930), writes about the Sophoclean tragic hero that his achievement illustrates for us "... an inner citadel where we may rule our own spirits; live as free men; die without dishonoring humanity" (189).

A tiny book consisting of three lectures by noted Greek scholar H. D. F. Kitto offers a clear and erudite (also indispensable and entertaining) discussion of all the great issues associated with Greek tragedy. In *Sophocles: Dramatist & Philosopher* (1958), he helpfully defines the gods (for modern audiences) as "being simply those aspects and conditions of life which we have to accept because we can not change them" (1). These are harsh words for those of us who behave as if we are fully in charge of our lives. Contemplated soberly, they are also reassuring words. Without a sense of underlying stability and order against which we measure ourselves, life is chaos. Kitto writes:

> ... Teiresias ... can ... prophesy [because] the events with which [he deals] are not random ones; certain observable laws underlie them. A racing-tipster on the other hand cannot prophesy; he can only guess—and I may remind you that the Modern Greek for *the horse* [is the same for] 'the irrational'. Prophecy, in Sophocles—and in Shakespeare too—is the denial of chaos. (55)

On the question of guilt and responsibility, there is no consensus about Oedipus.

Scholars (E. R. Dodds is among the most interesting and most adamant) do not regard Oedipus as a bad man who "deserves" his punishment. Not only were his acts done unwittingly, in his murder of Laius, he was not the aggressor. But he was not solely a compassionate and masterful ruler; when his own power was threatened he became suspicious, impatient, hasty, imperious, and self-absorbed. He even threatened an insignificant servant with torture. The play is dense with compelling and inscrutable elements, but one way to understand Oedipus and his suffering is not to see it as a discrete event in the world, which would require that we question its justice, but to see it as a reflection of what *is*. Kitto writes:

> There has been a long drought; animals and crops are dying for lack of moisture. At last the rain comes—and

how does it come? Your Romantic poet will write of the gentle rain that falls from Heaven like a redeeming benison on the parched land—and certainly Heaven will sometimes oblige him by doing it like this; but as often as not the drought ends in violent storms: houses are struck by lightning, trees are uprooted, corn is beaten flat and spoiled, the bodies of drowned sheep float down the Severn. This is *true*; ... the gods do behave like this—and the man who says in consequence that these gods are evil and undeserving of our worship, or that, being evil, they are false gods—that man is a fool. They may not command our love; Aristotle remarked that if a man should say 'I love Zeus' you would find it very odd; but they must command our respect, and if we are wise we shall accommodate ourselves as well as we can to what we may know of their laws. (51)

Of course there are plenty of readers and scholars who will see these ideas differently. And these ideas are not all there is to say about Oedipus and Greek tragedy. The shelves of academic libraries are full of books just on Sophocles and his Theban plays. The subject is old—and inexhaustible.

Works Cited

Ahl, Frederick. *Sophocles Oedipus: Evidence and Self-Conviction*. Ithaca: Cornell University Press, 1991.

Budelmann, Felix. *The Language of Sophocles*. Cambridge University Press, 2000.

Collins, Clifton. *Sophocles*. Edinburgh: W. Blackwood, 1871.

Dodds, E. R. "On Misunderstanding the *Oedipus Rex*." in *Twentieth Century Views of "Oedipus Rex."* Michael John O'Brien, Ed. Englewood Cliffs, N.J: Prentice Hall Trade, 1968.

Easterling, P. E. *The Cambridge Companion to Greek Tragedy*. New York: Cambridge University Press, 1997.

Gardiner, Cynthia P. *The Sophoclean Chorus*. Iowa City: University of Iowa Press, 1987.

Hamilton, Edith. *The Greek Way to Western Civilization*, 1930.

Jebb, R. C. *Sophocles: Oedipus Tyrannus*. Cambridge: Cambridge University Press, 1893.

Kitto, H. D. F. *Sophocles: Dramatist & Philosopher*. London: Oxford University Press, 1958.

Knox, Bernard. *Oedipus at Thebes*. New Haven: Yale University Press, 1957.

———. *The Heroic Temper*. Berkeley: University of California Press, 1964.

Meineck, Peter and Paul Woodruff. *Theban Plays*. Hackett Publishing Company, 2003.

Musurillo, Herbert. *The Light and the Darkness*. Leiden: E. J. Brill, 1967.

Raphael, D. D. "Why Does Tragedy Please?" in *Tragedy: Vision and Form*. Robert W. Corrigan, Ed. San Francisco: Chandler Pub. Co., 1965.

Rocco, Christopher. *Tragedy and Enlightenment*. Berkeley: University of California Press, 1997.

Scodel, Ruth. *Sophocles*. Boston: Twayne Publishers, 1984.

Whitman, Cedric H. *The Heroic Paradox*. Ithaca: Cornell University Press, 1982.

Zimmerman, Bernard. *Greek Tragedy: An Introduction*. Baltimore: Johns Hopkins University Press, 1991.

Critical Views

CLIFTON W. COLLINS ON SHIFTS IN PERSPECTIVE FROM AESCHYLUS TO SOPHOCLES

The generation of Aeschylus—stout warriors who had fought at Marathon, and sturdy seamen who "knew nothing" (as Aristophanes said) "except to call for barley-cake, and shout 'yo-heave-ho'"—had been content to believe implicitly all that Homer and their poets had taught them; and seeing around them traces of some mysterious force whose agency and purpose they were powerless to explain, they made a god of this Necessity or Destiny, and called it Nemesis. She was, in truth, a jealous deity, causing the rich and prosperous to founder like a vessel on a sunken reef,[1] and in one short day changing their joy to sorrow,—striking them pitilessly down in the plenitude of their grandeur, as a child in mere wantonness strikes down the tallest poppies in the corn-field. It was in vain to attempt to coax or cajole this capricious power by tears or offerings. History had taught men the futility of such bribes. Polycrates had thrown his precious ring into the sea; Croesus had filled the treasury of Delphi with his gold; but "no sacrifice or libation could save a man's soul from Death," and "on Death alone, of all divinities, Persuasion had no power."[2] And Herodotus, the most pious of historians, draws the obvious moral from the downfall of kings and the collapse of empires. "Envy," he says, "clings to all that mortal is.... Even a god cannot escape from Destiny."[3]

Such was the "tremendous creed" of which Aeschylus was a fitting exponent; with him the Furies are the satellites of Fate, and it is their eternal duty to pursue the murderer till death and after death.

(...)

Gradually the Greek mind expanded. The seas "were opened, commerce increased, men travelled far and saw

69

much; and thus the same stimulus was given to national thought and feeling by maritime enterprise as to the Jews under Solomon, and to the English under Elizabeth.[4] And as the Athenians grew adventurous, so they grew self-reliant. They doubted and questioned where they had before been content to shudder and believe. They attributed more to themselves and less to the blind agency of Destiny; and thus, in this progress of rationalism, there ensued that momentous change in thought represented by the transition in history from Herodotus to Thucydides, and in poetry from Aeschylus to Sophocles.

With this new generation, man is no longer bound hand and foot, powerless to move against his inevitable doom. He has liberty of choice in action, and by his knowledge or his ignorance, by his virtues or his vices, has made himself what he is. It is not so much a malignant power tormenting men in sheer envy at their wealth or happiness; but it is men themselves, who "play the fool with the times, while the spirits of the wise sit in the clouds and mock them." A long train of disastrous consequences often follows from a single impious speech or guilty deed—nay, even from a hot word or a hasty blow. Thus the idea of Destiny passes into that of retribution. Punishment surely follows sin, if not in a man's own day, yet descending, like an heirloom of misery, upon his children.

> "In life there is a seesaw; if we shape
> Our actions to our humours, other hands
> May shape their consequences to our pain.[5]

(...)

In each of [Sophocles'] plays he shows how passion works out its own end—whether it be the pride of Oedipus, the stubbornness of Creon, the insane fury of Ajax, or the jealousy of Dejanira. All these passions are simple and natural; there are no eccentricities of genius, no abnormal mental states, such as furnish the material of the modern drama. The Greek would not have understood the melancholy of Hamlet or the madness of Lear; still less would he have entered into the spirit of Timon's declaration,—

"I am misanthropos, and hate mankind."

Notes

1. Aesch., Eumen. 565.
2. Aesch., Fragm. of Niobe.
3. Hist. i. 35, 91; vii 46.
4. See Stanley's Lectures on the Jewish Church, ii. 186; Froude's History of England, viii. 426.
5. So says Sophocles, Ajax, 1085 (translated in Mr D'Arcy Thompson's 'Sales Attici'), anticipating the well-known words of Shakespeare:—

"The gods are just, and of our pleasant vices
Make instruments to scourge us."
—King Lear, Act v. sc. 3.

C. M. BOWRA ON RIGHT AND WRONG IN SOPHOCLES

[Sophocles uses] final song, divinities on the stage, and impartial human characters [to] guide us through the plays and to see events in their right light. But they do not disclose everything that the poet felt or tell us all that we wish to know or confirm all that we feel when the plays are acted. They are subsidiary to something else which is harder to define and yet more important, the way in which the plays force us to strong feelings and even to definite opinions and judgements about the characters and events. In the *Antigone*, for instance, we are made to feel that in the last resort Antigone is right to do as she does. Her nobility moves us, and her defence is far more touching and convincing than Creon's accusations. In due course we find that our feelings are justified. The gods punish Creon, and the Chorus at the end condemn him. But long before these revelations we are sure of our feelings and condemn Creon as we admire Antigone. Again, in the *Philoctetes*, where the issues are far more tangled and obscure, our feeling that Neoptolemus is wrong to do what Odysseus tells him and right to disobey him even in the face of what seems to be a divine plan are justified in the end, but we do not wait for the end to belie it. These feelings are forced on us not by what the characters say in their own defence but by what they are and by what they do. We react to them not merely with our intellects but with our hearts and consciences. We feel that it is unjust for Antigone to be treated as she is, that Neoptolemus is right not to tell lies, no matter for how important an end. In different ways this is true of all the plays. In each there are characters who appeal more to us than others and seem to have right on their side. We cannot always prove it during the play, but at the end we see that our feelings are justified.

It may seem rash to speak of right and wrong in a tragedy. There are forms of tragic suffering where such distinctions do not exist, where all that matters is the suffering of human beings. There are others, like Racine's *Britannicus*, which display great forces of evil at work but allow no clear distinction between right and wrong. Agrippine is indeed Nero's victim, but she is no virtuous woman and her troubles are the fruit of her own past crimes. The situation is different in Shakespeare. When Desdemona is ruined through the machinations of Iago or Macbeth driven to murder by his wife, we may distinguish between good and evil and feel as much hostility for the wicked as pity for their victims. But in the onrush of overwhelming emotions which he awakes we hardly wait to assess the balance of right and wrong, at least while we read or see the tragedy. Sophocles is not like this. The tragic emotions are as great as in Shakespeare; the excitement of the action is hardly less great. But in all the excitement and horror there is an element which is absent from Shakespeare. The tragic events are such that we inevitably try to explain them to ourselves and to find out how the poet explains them.

The reason of this is that while the conflict in Shakespeare is between men and men, in Sophocles it arises in the last analysis between men and gods. It is the gods who make Ajax mad, who ordain his hideous end for Heracles, who punish Creon, who arrange the whole career of Oedipus, who send Orestes to kill his mother, who decide that Philoctetes shall take Troy, who turn the old Oedipus into a daemonic being. When they are at work, the whole setting is different from Shakespeare's. It is in some sense theological, and if the gods act in this or that way, we ask why they do and what it means. We can hardly do otherwise, and Sophocles demands such questions from us; for he has his answers to them. To understand his tragic pattern we must understand his theology. It is a product of his age, and we know something about it. The difficulty is to find his own treatment of accepted doctrines in his presentation of particular issues. The chief evidence is what happens. When the gods intervene or display their will through oracles or prophets, we know what they mean and what their part is. In every play this happens. Some of the machinery may mean little or nothing to us. It is, for instance, hard to attach great importance to oracles. But, whatever Sophocles may have thought about them in ordinary life, and there is a good possibility that he believed in them, in his plays they account for a great deal, and that is all that concerns us. The plays are nearly all that we have of his and certainly all that matters. They show that Sophocles built his tragic conflicts on the relations of men with the gods, and therefore we must know what these relations are and mean.

Because of this, issues of right and wrong are more emphatic in Sophocles than in Shakespeare. If the gods force a fate on men, we ask not only why they do it but if they are right and if their victims deserve it. The question may not always be relevant, but we cannot but ask it, and Sophocles evidently intended that we should. Thus in his treatment of Oedipus, though he does not allow that Oedipus' hideous misfortunes are in any sense deserved, he knows that some will think that they are and has his answer for them. In the *Ajax* and *Antigone* the fall of Ajax and Creon follows a traditional scheme and is by Greek standards deserved. In the *Electra* and *Philoctetes* the issue is much less clear. Until the action is quite advanced we may wonder whether Electra is really right to desire vengeance on her mother or whether the gods' plan to bring Philoctetes to Troy is really right, but in the end we see that what the gods approve is right and must be accepted. This interest in rights and wrongs is an essential part of the play's effect on us. Because our moral emotions are aroused, we are more excited about what happens. The conflict between right and wrong, its obscurities and its excitements, is fundamental to Sophoclean tragedy.

This interest touches more than the mere structure of a play or its main theme. The chief characters sometimes argue and disagree on right and wrong as they do not in Shakespeare. The burial of Polynices is a matter for bitter disagreement not only between Antigone and Creon but between Antigone and Ismene; Deianira's attempt to win back Heracles by magic is viewed differently by the Chorus, by Hyllus, and by Heracles; Odysseus and Neoptolemus do not see eye to eye about the uses of deceit for political ends; the old Oedipus argues fiercely with Creon about his alleged crimes. In these controversies passions are aroused and are undeniably dramatic, but the issue has to be settled and is a matter of morals. In Euripides debates on such points are no less common. Jason and Medea, Dionysus and Pentheus, represent opposite causes and apply rhetoric and sophistry to them. But in Sophocles the subjects of dispute seem simpler and more fundamental. The interest is less in the give and take of debate than in the importance of what is at stake. Euripides may not always care which side we support; Sophocles clearly cares a great deal and, though he is always dramatic, he leads us to a decision. With him actual argument counts less than it does with Euripides. His debates and disputes appeal first to the conscience and to the heart. He wishes to convince us in all our being, to carry us with him in a full and imaginative understanding of what is at stake.

It may then be said that there is in all Sophocles' plays an element of ethical discussion, of casuistry, which pervades the atmosphere and gives meaning to the tragic events. As his art developed, these issues became more complex and more subtle. In the early plays they are quite simply and directly presented, but in the later plays, notably in the *Electra* and *Philoctetes*, they are so complex that much of the excitement lies in finding out what they are. The protagonists in a struggle no longer stand on opposite sides of right and wrong but seem to present such a struggle in themselves. As he grew older, Sophocles did not abate his love of an ethical issue but brought it closer to the complexities of human nature. But in all the plays the dramatic material demands close considerations of right and wrong. They are forced on us, and we cannot neglect them. This does not mean that Sophocles is didactic or instructional in any narrow or derogatory sense, that he uses his characters simply to illustrate moral truths. He is always a dramatist, and the ethical issues are subordinated to human interests. But just as it is impossible to understand human life without considering moral issues and even passing moral judgements, so in Sophoclean tragedy much of the interest turns on such issues. Sophocles is as much concerned with men's souls as with their fortunes.

It is perhaps in this that his peculiar difficulty lies. In the scheme of every play there is a moral or religious problem, an issue to which there must be a right answer but on which more than one opinion is tenable. This issue is presented in a very personal and concrete form, with all the richness that great art can give. As in life we may be deceived and form wrong opinions about matters of great moment, so in his plays Sophocles shows how deceptive many issues are, presents different views of them, and looks at them from more than one angle. As the drama develops, the nature of the problem becomes clearer, and eventually we know what it is. It follows that in examining his work we must find what these problems are and how they are presented. If we can do this, we have made a considerable advance in the study of his work and art.

(...)

By modern standards the gods who decide on Oedipus' fate before he is born and then inflict it on him without mercy treat him cruelly. But this is not a view that Sophocles would have held or admitted. He would more probably hold that men cannot judge the gods and might even agree with Heraclitus that 'For God all things are beautiful and good and just, but men think some things unjust and others just.' For he states emphatically that the gods must be honoured, and shows that their word must be believed. Nor is it legitimate to argue that their word is sometimes hard to understand. That, too, arises from the ignorance and blindness in which man lives. He can only do his best to understand the gods by what means he possesses, to recognize that his own judgement may be wrong. The gods, who know everything, are right. Nor may man complain of them. He must humble himself before them and admit that he is nothing and that he knows nothing. This is the lesson of *King Oedipus*. The last words draw attention to it. Oedipus is

That Mighty King, who knew the riddle's mystery.

But his knowledge is of no avail in dealing with the mysteries of the gods. On this note of ignorance and humiliation the play ends. It is hardly a quiet end. Oedipus is still an abhorred and defiled creature who may not remain in the daylight and is fated to suffer more. Creon, who does correctly what the gods require, insists on his going indoors. His manner may seem rigorous, but he does his religious duty. He cannot do otherwise, and Oedipus, now fully conscious of his nothingness before the gods, knows that Creon is right. He asks to be sent out of the land (1518); he knows that the gods abhor him (1518). What will happen next must, as Creon sees (1438–9), wait on the gods' decision. We know that Teiresias has prophesied more miseries for Oedipus and that they will infallibly come. The play ends in the anguish of humiliation and the anticipation of more to come. But at last the truth is out, and the gods have had their way.

The gods humble Oedipus as a lesson to men not to trust in their happiness or their knowledge. The horror of his fate and his fall is fore-ordained that others may learn from it. But though this plan determines all that happens, the actual events follow a pattern which is tragic and Sophoclean. When Oedipus kills his father and marries his mother the inviolable laws of the gods are broken and the divine order of things sustains a grievous wound. The wound must be healed, the order restored. Before this can be done, the evil that has been, albeit unconsciously, committed, must show its full force. This it does in the growth of Oedipus' illusions when the plague forces a crisis on him. From illusions he moves to dangerous acts. His fits of fury, his moments of scepticism, his certainty that he is right, are the natural products of his state. Such a condition cannot last, and it is broken by the events which follow the death of Polybus. As Oedipus comes to see the truth and to punish himself for his past actions, he makes his peace with the gods. He does what is right, accepts his position, knows the truth. Through resignation and suffering the rightful harmony of things is restored. By divine standards Oedipus at the end of the play is a better man than at the beginning. His humiliation is a lesson both to others and to him. Democritus' words, 'the foolish learn modesty in misfortune', may be applied to Oedipus, who has indeed been foolish in his mistakes and illusions and has been taught modesty through suffering. The lesson which the gods convey through his fall is all the more impressive because he is the great king and the great man that he is. In the eyes of the gods what matters is that he should know who and what he really is. To secure this end his power and his glory must be sacrificed. In his acceptance of his fall, his readiness to take part in it, Oedipus shows a greatness nobler than when he read the riddle of the Sphinx and became king of Thebes.

H. D. F. Kitto on the Problem of "Justice"

Finally, in my list of misleading translations, there is our word 'Justice'. It is our rendering of the word *Dikê*, and some times it is not far wrong. In my own translation of the *Electra* I used it occasionally, *faute de mieux*; sometimes, when justice would have been quite wrong, I used 'retribution', even though that was not quite right. In order to show that this is a point of substance, not mere pedantry, I will cite a passage from the *Oedipus Rex*. Oedipus has at last discovered the awful truth: he has already killed his father and married his mother. The killing of Laius was not, as presented in the play, wanton murder:

if Oedipus had not lashed out at the irascible old man in the chariot, the old man would have killed him. Sophocles avoids any suggestion that Oedipus was seriously to blame, either for this or for the marriage. But when Oedipus has discovered the truth, and so has brought himself under his own curse, the chorus observes: 'Time has found you out, and is submitting you to justice for your incestuous marriage.' If we suppose that this is what the chorus actually *says*, we are puzzled or even indignant with Sophocles: how can it be 'justice', that a man is so savagely punished for what he did in complete ignorance? I do not know what view an English law-court would take if in these circumstances a man were arraigned for parricide and incest, but I feel confident that its idea of justice would be much more merciful than this. If so, does it mean that we have advanced in civilization? No; all it means is that we have mistranslated the Greek.

(...)

'Justice' is a good word; *dikê* is neutral. 'Justice' is a moral word; *dikê* may be nothing of the sort. For instance, philosophers not much older than Sophocles had begun to formulate ideas about the physical universe. One idea, naturally, was that underneath its apparent variability there lies a basic regularity: for example, the orbit of the sun year by year is perfectly regular—why? One philosopher, Anaximander, wrote about the fairly obvious fact that Nature preserves a balance. As we have his remark only in a quotation, with no context, we do not know precisely what he had in mind, but evidently it involved the idea that in the long run things even out. If we say that action and reaction are equal, or speak of things like 'mean rainfall', we are giving a specific expression to the same general truth. And how did these writers express these ideas? Quite naturally, by using the work *dikê* and its opposite *adikia*.

(...)

I have been speaking of the physical universe only, but the Greeks [made the mistake of extending] the general laws of the physical universe to that other universe, the world of human action and passion. We, being wiser, make the opposite mistake of separating the two completely; we know a lot about the laws which operate in the one, and suppose, being irreligious, that there are no comparable laws in the other, so that when things go wrong, instead of asking what laws we have contravened, we blame the Labour Party or the Conservative Party. It is insufficiently recognized by political theorists that this is the great advantage conferred on us by our party system. In the Greek conception, *dikê* works both universes. The law which I put in the specific and modern form that action and reaction are equal applies here too. Other formulae could be devised, but the basic idea is that *dikê*, the regular order of things, may be contravened for a time, but in the end it must reassert itself. *Adikia* is by its very nature unstable.

This, I believe, is the core of Sophocles' religious thinking. Naturally, there is more than this, but before going farther I will ask if it does not already lighten some of our difficulties. Oedipus has committed parricide and incest; that is to say, he has greatly offended against two of the fundamental laws, or fundamental sanctities, of human life. But he did it in all innocence?—not, for example, like Creon in the *Antigone*, who offended against comparable sanctities deliberately, from sheer unwisdom. Certainly; but if, in all innocence, a man eats potassium cyanide, thinking that it is sugar, his innocence and ignorance will not save him. The gods who order these things will not be moved; as the chorus in the *Agamemnon* says, 'Neither by libations nor by sacrifice will you bend the inflexible will of the gods.' Life can be cruel, but we had better not try to deceive ourselves. 'Gods', as the simple Huntsman said in the Hippolytus, 'ought to be more understanding than men.' Perhaps they are, but they do not forgive nor make exceptions.

But the play does not end with the proof of divine omniscience and human ignorance. It ends, as it begins, with Oedipus. "Equal to zero"—the chorus' estimate, proposed at the moment when Oedipus learns who he is, seems right and indeed inevitable. But it is hard to accept. It means that the heroic action of Oedipus, with all that his action is made to represent, is a hollow mockery, a snare and a delusion. It suggests that man should not seek, for fear of what he will find. It renounces the qualities and actions which distinguish man from the beasts, and accepts a state of blind, mute acquiescence no less repugnant to the human spirit than the recklessness demanded by Jocasta's universe of chance. And yet at that moment it seems the only possible conclusion. With Oedipus as their paradigm, it is difficult to see what other estimate the chorus can make.

A different estimate is proposed, not in words but in dramatic action, by the final scene of the play. For Oedipus, the paradigm, on whom the chorus' despairing estimate is based, surmounts the catastrophe and reasserts himself. He is so far from being equal to zero that in the last lines of the play Creon has to tell him not to try to "rule in everything" (1522). This last scene of the play, so often criticized as anticlimactic or unbearable, is on the contrary vital for the play, and a development which makes its acceptance possible. It shows us the recovery of Oedipus, the reintegration of the hero, the reconstitution of the imperious, dynamic, intelligent figure of the opening scenes.

This is an astonishing development, for Oedipus, when he comes out of the palace, is so terrible a sight that the chorus cannot bear to look at him (1303), and his situation is such that the chorus expresses a wish that it had never known him (1348). It approves his wish that he could have died on the mountainside before he reached manhood (1356), and tells him that he would be better dead now than alive and blind (1368).

This despair is reflected in the words of Oedipus himself: they are the words of a broken man.

The first lines present us with an Oedipus who speaks in terms we can hardly recognize: he speaks of his movements, voice, and destiny as things alien to him, utterly beyond his control. "Where am I being carried? How does my voice fly about, carried aloft? O my destiny, to what point have you leaped out?" (1309–11).[2] These are the words of a blinded man awakening to the realization of his terrible impotence, but they express also a feeling that Oedipus is no loner an active force but purely passive. This impression is enforced by his next words, an address to the darkness in which he will now forever move, and a reference to the pain which pierces his eyes and mind, alike (1313–18). The climax of this unnatural passivity is reached when Oedipus first becomes aware of the presence of the chorus (1321). His realization takes the form of a grateful recognition of their steadfastness in "looking after the blind man" (1323). This is an expression of his utter dependency on others; he is so far from action now that he needs help even to exist. He seems indeed a zero, equal to nothing.

It is precisely at this point that the chorus reminds us, and him, that part at any rate of his present calamitous state, his blindness, is his own choice, the result of his own independent action after the recognition of the truth. This was not called for by the prophecy of Apollo, nor was it demanded in the oracle's instructions about the murderer's punishment or the curse on him pronounced by Oedipus. It was Oedipus' autonomous action, and the chorus now asks him why he did it: "You have done dreadful things" (*deina drasas*, 1327). They use the word for action which was peculiarly his when he was *tyrannos*, and the question they ask him suggests an explanation. "Which of the divinities spurred you on?" Oedipus' reply defends his action and rejects the chorus' formula, which would shift the responsibility for the blinding off his shoulders. Apollo, he says, brought my sufferings to fulfilment, but "as for the hand that struck my eyes, it was mine and no one else's" (1330–31). He confirms what the messenger has already told us; the action was "self-chosen" (*authairetoi*, 1231), and a few lines later the chorus reproves him for it. It was in fact an action typical of Oedipus *tyrannos*, one which anticipated the reaction, advice, and objection of others, a *fait accompli*, a swift decisive act for which he assumes full responsibility and which he proceeds to defend. And now, as if the chorus' reminder of his own action had arrested the disintegration of his personality which was so terribly clear in the first speech after his entrance, the old Oedipus reappears. As he rejects the chorus' suggestion that the responsibility was not his, grounds his action logically, and (as his lines make the transition from the lyric of lamentation to the iambic of rational speech) rejects their reproaches, all the traits of his magnificent character reappear. It is not long before he is recognizably the same man as before.

He is still the man of decisive action, and still displays the courage which had always inspired that action. His attitude to the new and terrible situation in which he now finds himself is full of the same courage which he displayed before: he accepts the full consequences of the curse he imposed on himself, and insists stubbornly, in the face of Creon's opposition, that he be put to death or exiled from Thebes. He brushes aside the compromise offered by Creon with the same courage that dismissed the attempts of Tiresias, Jocasta, and the herdsman to stop the investigation. The speed and impatience of his will is if anything increased; *tachys*, "swift," is still his word. "Take me away from this place as quickly as possible" (*hoti tachista*, 1340). "Hide me away as quickly as possible" (*hopôs tachista*, 1410). "Throw me out of this land as quickly as may be" (*hoson tachisth'*, 1436).

As before, he has no patience with half-measures or delay; the oracle and his own curse call for his exile or death, and he sees nothing to be gained by prolonging the inaction. The same analytical intelligence is at work; he is right, and, as we know, Creon finally does late what Oedipus wanted done early—he exiles Oedipus from Thebes. The same hard intelligence which insisted on full clarity and all the facts is displayed in his remorseless exploration and formulation of the frightful situation in which he finds himself. He spares himself no detail of the consequences of his pollution for himself and for his daughters. It is typical that while Creon's reaction is to cover and conceal (1426 ff.), Oedipus brings everything out into the open, analyzing in painful detail his own situation and that of his children. The intelligence of Oedipus is at work even at the high pitch of semi-hysterical grief;[3] even in his outburst of lamentation he distinguishes between what he regards as the gods' responsibility and his own. And an extraordinary thing emerges as Oedipus abandons the wild lament of his first reaction for the reasoned speech of the last part of the play: it becomes apparent that even the self-blinding was based on the deliberation and reflection which in Oedipus *tyrannos* always preceded action.[4] To the chorus' reproach that he had "made a bad decision" (1367) in blinding himself he replies with the old impatience and a touch of the old anger. "Do not read me a lesson or give me any advice, to the effect that I have not done the best thing" (1369–70). And he goes on to describe in detail the reasoning by which he arrived at the decision to put out his eyes (1370–83). Sophocles makes it clear that this is an account of past reflection preceding the action (and not a present rationalization of it) by his use of the past tense throughout the speech.[5] Oedipus is fully confident of the rightness of the action and the thought which preceded and produced it. And all through this scene he maps out the future for himself and his family, giving Creon instructions for the burial of Jocasta, his own expulsion from Thebes, and the upbringing of his sons and daughters.

Notes

2. (…) "in the manner of that which is carried." Jebb comments: "He feels as if his voice was borne from him on the air in a direction over which he has no control."

3. For which the medium is the lyric meter of his opening song after his reappearance on stage: he does not return to the iambic medium of rational speech until he begins to argue in 1369.

4. For the blinding as "deliberate purpose" see Sir Richard Livingstone, "The Exodos of the *Oedipus Tyrannus*," in *Greek Poetry and Life* (Oxford, 1936), p. 160.

5. (…) 1385. What Oedipus says now about what he thought then is proved exact by the messenger's account of what he said at the time (1271–74).

E. R. Dodds on Oedipus as a Free Agent

But what is the alternative? If Oedipus is the innocent victim of a doom which he cannot avoid, does this not reduce him to a mere puppet? Is not the whole play a 'tragedy of destiny' which denies human freedom? This is the second of the heresies which I set out to refute. Many readers have fallen into it, Sigmund Freud among them;[4] and you can find it confidently asserted in various popular handbooks, some of which even extend the assertion to Greek tragedy in general—thus providing themselves with a convenient label for distinguishing Greek from 'Christian' tragedy. But the whole notion is in fact anachronistic. The modern reader slips into it easily because we think of two clear-cut alternative views—either we believe in free will or else we are determinists. But fifth-century Greeks did not think in these terms any more than Homer did: the debate about determinism is a creation of Hellenistic thought. Homeric heroes have their predetermined 'portion of life'; they must die on their 'appointed day'; but it never occurs to the poet or his audience that this prevents them from being free agents. Nor did Sophocles intend that it should occur to readers of the *Oedipus Rex*. Neither in Homer nor in Sophocles does divine foreknowledge of certain events imply that all human actions are predetermined. If explicit confirmation of this is required, we have only to turn to lines 1230 f., where the Messenger emphatically distinguishes Oedipus' self-blinding as 'voluntary' and 'self-chosen' from the 'involuntary' parricide and incest. Certain of Oedipus' past actions were fate-bound; but everything that he does on the stage from first to last he does as a free agent.

Even in calling the parricide and the incest 'fate-bound' I have perhaps implied more than the average Athenian of Sophocles' day would have recognized. As A. W. Gomme put it, 'the gods know the future, but they do not order it: they know who will win the next Scotland and England football match, but that does not alter the fact that the victory will depend on the skill, the determination, the fitness of the players, and a little on luck'.[5] That may not satisfy the analytical philosopher, but it seems to have satisfied the ordinary man at all periods. Bernard Knox aptly quotes the prophecy of Jesus to St. Peter, 'Before the cock crow, thou shalt deny me thrice.' The Evangelists clearly did not intend to imply that Peter's subsequent action was 'fate-bound' in the sense that he could not have chosen otherwise; Peter fulfilled the prediction, but he did so by an act of free choice.[6]

In any case I cannot understand Sir Maurice Bowra's[7] idea that the gods *force* on Oedipus the knowledge of what he has done. They do nothing of the kind; on the contrary, what fascinates us is the spectacle of a man freely choosing, from the highest motives, a series of actions which lead to his own ruin. Oedipus might have left the plague to take its course; but pity for the sufferings of his people compelled him to consult Delphi. When Apollo's word came back, he might still have left the murder of Laius uninvestigated; but piety and justice required him to act. He need not have forced the truth from the reluctant Theban herdsman; but because he cannot rest content with a lie, he must tear away the last veil from the illusion in which he has lived so long. Teiresias, Jocasta, the herdsman, each in turn tries to stop him, but in vain: he must read the last riddle, the riddle of his own life. The immediate cause of Oedipus' ruin is not 'Fate' or 'the gods'—no oracle said that he must discover the truth—and still less does it lie in his own weakness; what causes his ruin is his own strength and courage, his loyalty to Thebes, and his loyalty to the truth. In all this we are to see him as a free agent: hence the suppression of the hereditary curse. And his self-mutilation and self-banishment are equally free acts of choice.

Notes
4. Sigmund Freud, *The Interpretation of Dreams* (London, Modern Library, 1938), 108.

5. A. W. Gomme, *More Essays in Greek History and Literature* (Oxford, 1962), 211.

6. B. M. W. Knox, *Oedipus at Thebes* (Yale, 1957), 39.

7. C. M. Bowra, *Sophoclean Tragedy* (Oxford, 1944), ch. v.

Very subtly is the theme of the plague united with the symbolism of the ship. The priest of Zeus, narrating to Oedipus the latest ravages of the common disease, speaks of the city as a ship (23–4) that

Cannot keep its prow above the bloody swell.

It is wallowing in blood, in death, as the bodies fall in the city and empty the state of its manpower (55–7), the ship of its crew. But the pilot Oedipus—as Jocasta is later to call him (923) and the Chorus in a moment of eulogy describes him (694–6)—tells the priest and the suppliants that he has not been asleep (65–7),

But know you that I have wept many tears
And travelled many roads within my mind.

That is, he has been worried and deeply concerned—a characteristic mark of Oedipus' make-up. He began his career by wandering out of anxiety away from Corinth where he was raised; and his final wandering will take him back in spirit to discover the mystery of his birth and birthmark. Indeed, the theme of Oedipus the wanderer, the outcast from birth (1350), whose nurse and mother is the broad range of Mt. Cithaeron (1090–95), is a minor, secondary one within the broad and rich background of the play. It is to Cithaeron that he wishes to return, to live and die as a recluse among the hills (1451 ff.), Cithaeron that heard his baby cries and echoed, at the end, with his animal bellow of recognition as he sees the truth of what the prophet had foretold.

But it is with the ship and harbor imagery that I am chiefly concerned. To Jocasta, the Chorus and Creon, Oedipus is the pilot who has steered the ship of state on a fair breeze; and Oedipus himself is conscious of his administrative role. Indeed, he is not like the Creon of the *Antigone* who sees his captaincy as a kind of divine absolutism, a role which gives him complete dominion over the citizens as though they were his slaves. No, Oedipus fulfills his position by his positive contribution to the welfare of the state, and his actions always depend upon the consultation of the Theban people. It is precisely his solicitude which helps to bring him to disaster. His position begins to disintegrate with the reluctant arrival of Teiresias. Oedipus cannot imagine the reason why the ancient seer will not speak out and suspects that Creon and Teiresias have guilty knowledge of Laius' death. Very rightly does Oedipus conclude that kings most often lose their thrones by the machinations of those who are closest to them; if Creon and the prophet got rid of Laius, they surely now would try to murder his successor. Teiresias' withering reply unleashes all the most shocking details of Oedipus' unwitting crime, clothed in prophetic obscurity. He tells him of the dread-footed Curse that is pursuing him (419 ff.).

> Both now while you have sight, and later blind.
> And what harbor shall there not be for your cry,
> What Cithaeron's grove shall not re-echo with it,
> When you realize the marriage which you've made,
> Sailing on a favorable breeze to a harborless harbor ...

Oedipus' great and sudden rise in life, his towering success as king of Thebes—this is the harbor into which he has piloted his ship under favorable winds. Teiresias' words recall the pathetic prayer of the Chorus in the parodos (194 ff.): they beseech their patron gods to drive out Ares the fever-god (whom they believe is at fault for the plague), like an infectious, disease-bearing cloud, to the east or to the west,

> to Amphitrite's great chamber,
> Or that most friendless anchorage,
> The Thracian sea.

To Oedipus, then, the palace of Thebes has become a "friendless anchorage," a treacherous harbor which consumes and destroys the vessels that are innocently moored in it. The fair breeze, the brief success in quelling the baneful influence of the Sphinx, the solemn nuptials with queen Jocasta—all this was but the semblance of happiness, a shadowy glory sent by the gods to make Oedipus' descent into the abyss all the more appalling and irreversible.

But there is a still more ominous pronouncement to come. The Chorus ironically interprets Oedipus' voyage in the ode which just follows the final revelation (1186 ff.). We see now that the rise-and-fall pattern of human life not only fits those who are guilty of *hybris* as they had previously suggested (873 ff.); it may also describe the life of any man whom the gods have somehow chosen to humiliate, thrusting him into a life which is merely an illusion of happiness, and then plunging him into the blackest despair.[1] This image of climbing and falling we shall touch upon farther on. What is interesting in this last choral ode is the final development of the ship and harbor imagery which had been so pervasive throughout the earlier part of the play. For the earlier cry of healing, the paean, has turned into a lament (1219), as though Oedipus were already dead. In their most prophetic mood, the Chorus continues to sing (1207 ff.):

Alas, my famous Oedipus!
The same great harbor sufficed
Both for father and for son, to fall,
Both husbands. How, how indeed,
Could those maternal fields, poor child,
Have born you for so long?

The imagery, though obscurely delicate is direct. The harborless harbor, the friendless anchorage, is none other than his own mother. He has, like a grim husbandman, inherited the fields his father sowed—the Greek is ambiguous—and he has "fallen" upon the same harbor as his father.[2] It is the moment of supreme irony in the play: for the Greek for "harbor" can also mean "womb."[3] No greater crime can be imagined; no greater disturbance of the Laws which rule on high.

Notes

1. See my article, "The Illusion of Prosperity in Sophocles and Gregory of Nyssa," *Amer. Journal of Philology* 82 (1961), 182–187.

2. For a discussion of the many levels of irony in this word, see *Symbol and Myth in Ancient Poetry*, pp. 86–7.

3. See the fragment of Empedocles cited in Diels-Kranz, *Fragmente der Vorsokratiker* (7th ed. 3 vols. Berlin 1954), I.346.21. Aeschylus makes Polyneices "flee the darkness of his mother" (*Seven against Thebes* 664), that is, the womb.

DAVID SEALE ON THE STAGECRAFT OF THE OPENING SCENE

Oedipus the King opens with a movement, not a tableau.[1] Before a word is spoken a group of suppliants enters from a parodos and makes rapidly for the altars in front of the palace. The manner of their arrival bespeaks the earnestness of their supplication; they are in need of salvation. They are dressed in the traditional style of suppliants, in white tunics and cloaks, their hair bound in fillets, also of white. In their hands they are carrying olive branches, wreathed in wool, which they lay on the altars.[2] The composition of the whole gathering is made up from three separate groups which are later pointed out (16–19): children, chosen young men and aged priests, who perhaps marshal the others. This division into three groups was presumably reflected in the stage presentation[3] and seems to confirm that this initial entry was indeed a kind of formal procession. They all sit down by the altars where they have laid their olive branches, in the posture of supplication. The old priest, who is to be their spokesman and who likely led the procession, may remain standing—although initially, until he is called upon to speak, he too may be seated like his fellow suppliants. As this large movement comes to an end and the crowd settles there is an air of expectation.[4] Then, as if summoned by the silent throng, Oedipus, the king of Thebes, comes forth from the central door. Those at his feet press closely around him.

The visual relationship between the 'solitary'[5] standing figure and the prostrate assembly is immediately reinforced in a particular and striking way: 'Children ...' This, the first word of the tragedy, Oedipus addresses to young and old alike. On the one hand, it is a natural expression of the role which the presence of the suppliants confers upon him. He is the leader, the protector, the patriarch. On the other hand, there is the real father, the polluted one, who at the last is compelled to relinquish the daughters born of his own incest. The image of the father is the instant link between the external political circumstance and the lurking family horror. Oedipus' relationship with his 'children' begins and ends the drama.

Our first view of Oedipus, then, is of a man in the public eye, a beloved king who is sought by his people. This matching of the large group against the single figure provides the scenic background for the developing interplay between the public and the private domain. All that the words of the old priest make him, the wise monarch, the intellectual, the saviour, the almost god, is enhanced by the stage picture. And 'appearances' are founded in facts: this scene is a repeat, made visual, of a past calamity when the city was similarly 'cast down' and 'raised' by the wisdom of Oedipus. The outsider who solved the riddle of the Sphinx and became king is a man uniquely qualified to solve the current mystery of the plague.

But Oedipus' private past is no less prominent, uncannily and inextricably interwoven with the playing of the public part. When he appears before the waiting crowd he comes of his own accord, to be among his people and to hear their appeals in person (6–7). This 'instinctive' entry is consonant with the fact that, after the pretence of enquiry, he *already knows* the significance of their presence. But, ironically, this initial understanding of others' suffering leads directly to the unconscious intuition of his own doomed existence: he takes on the suffering of the entire city *as a personal belonging*. The identification is real and appalling; he is a native Theban, he is the monumental sufferer, his 'sickness' is their sickness. The public spectacle is suddenly a spectre of private disaster as the single figure 'absorbs' the mass of woe before him, as he becomes the true embodiment of the fallen city. Visually, the crowd which exalts him is also the measure of his ruin. Moreover Oedipus eradicates his own personal existence only to light upon it in the very adoption of the public stance. And this sets the pattern for nearly all his utterance in the early scenes; the public role makes him the unconscious voice of his own secrets.

In no other of the extant plays of Sophocles does the action open with a public ceremony. Even more remarkable is the contrast between the expectations of the myth and the first theatrical impression. The man with the most celebrated secret steps, unasked and unhesitating, into the limelight of a large open assembly. And the setting is more than a physical context; Oedipus understands it by instinct, he identifies with it, it is his conscious world. But the apparent splendour resonates with another more sinister meaning. This truth is no remote and buried thing, it is at hand in the public crisis, lying in wait for the man of public conscience, almost visible in the public gesturing. Illusion and reality co-exist under the same aspect, overlapping and confused the one with the other.[6] Every self-conscious response to the public situation opens up a recess of the private inner realm which, to the spectator's eye, more aptly and with increasing fascination fulfils the meaning of the stage presentation.

Notes

1. The question, much discussed, turns on whether the entry represents an arrival proper or a conventional expedient to allow the opening tableau to be formed, the so-called 'cancelled entry'. P. Burian, 'The Play before the Prologue: Initial Tableaux on the Greek Stage', *Ancient and Modern: Essays in Honour of G. F. Else* (University of Michigan Press, Ann Arbor, Mich., 1977), pp. 83–4, presents a convincing case for the complete stage presentation, which is fully formulated in the text as a ritual procession and which, as B. M. W. Knox has shown, *Oedipus at Thebes* (Yale University Press, New Haven, 1957), pp. 159–60, is dramatically of great significance; they come to Oedipus as to a god. The opening scene introduces an important ambiguity: the suppliants approach altars which are god's but also Oedipus' (16), and it is not made explicit at this point that one altar at least is Apollo's. At all events it is Oedipus who appears. The 'equation' with god is the first expression of a relationship which is

only truly revealed when Oedipus at the last acknowledges the divine master of his fate, in a cry which recognises Apollo (1329) and in the final return to the house, in which, hidden away, he must await the god's word. For a thorough discussion of the general problem of the 'cancelled entry' see O. Taplin, *The Stagecraft of Aeschylus* (Clarendon Press, Oxford, 1977), pp. 134–6.

2. R. C. Jebb's visualisation of the scene, in Jebb (ed.), *The Oedipus Tyrannus* (Cambridge University Press, Cambridge, 1893).

3. There has been a certain reluctance to accept the presence of a large assembly. The main concern is the inconvenience of the exit of too large a number just prior to the arrival of the Chorus. This inconvenience is overstressed, given the spaciousness of the Greek theatre. For the extreme view see W.M. Calder III, 'The Staging of the Prologue of *Oedipus Tyrannus*', *Phoenix*, vol. 13 (1959), pp. 121–9, who supposes that the audience was addressed from the stage as the people of Thebes, two mute boys being all that was required for the actual supplication. The notion of 'audience address' in the case of Greek tragedy has, however, been brought into serious doubt by D. Bain, 'Audience Address in Greek Tragedy', *Classical Quarterly*, n.s., vol. 25 (1975), pp. 13–25, whose arguments are further reinforced by Taplin, *Stagecraft of Aeschylus*, pp. 129–30. Most editors in fact accept the employment of a significant number of extras. But one word of caution is in order; clearly the group should not be larger than the Chorus that comes later as the representative body of the Theban people. On the question of composition, the text (16–19) has been suspected. See especially A.S. Henry, 'Sophocles, *Oedipus Tyrannus*: The Interpretation of the Opening Scene and The Text of l. 18', *Classical Quarterly*, n.s., vol. 17 (1967), pp. 48–51. The three divisions of age, however, are accepted by most editors and represent categories appropriate for supplication. It may be that the children are in the majority.

4. It is possible, as Burian suggests, 'The Play before the Prologue: Initial Tableaux on the Greek Stage', p. 83, that the spokesman of the group, the priest of Zeus, is given a prominence on-stage which might lead the audience to believe that he was there to open the proceedings. In this case the entry of Oedipus, unannounced as it is, would occur as something of a surprise.

5. There may be a retinue; Oedipus is a king and his wealth is not an insignificant aspect of his status. It is one of the three ideas apostrophised by Oedipus (380) and figures in the prophet's vision of the great reversal (455). But on-stage any attendants that Oedipus might have would not take away from the essential relationship of king and subjects.

6. The importance of this theme is the main concern of K. Reinhardt's brilliant study, *Sophocles*, trans. by H. and D. Harvey (Blackwell, Oxford, 1979), pp. 94–134.

CYNTHIA P. GARDINER ON THE CONTRIBUTION OF THE CHORUS

It is not at all surprising (...) that the chorus begin the song with a statement of faith, given their earlier prayers, their reliance upon the gods, and their statements of faith in the Delphic oracle. The audience may at once begin to suspect the chorus will discuss the new religious problem of the validity of oracles. The first strophe ends with a confirmation of the divine and eternal nature (872) of the High Laws of the universe; but the chorus do not define or specify these laws so as to lead the audience to think of any one (or more) of the actions that have been discussed or committed in the play so far. Then the antistrophe begins with *hybris*, which must surely have been understood as the breaking of the High Laws. This behavior, this vice, the chorus personify; they do not speak of the man who commits *hybris* but of the vice itself, the arrogant disregard of the High Laws that brings with it general destruction, although the struggle that benefits the general good is welcome (879–881). They claim to rely upon divine leadership (882). In this context, their meaning would seem obvious: *hybris* is bad for the city, but certain rivalry is good; the god must distinguish between them, striking down the bad but letting the useful continue.

The chorus go on to explain this more fully in the second strophe (883–896). If someone commits hubristic deeds— again they do not specify the particular deeds, and again they assume such acts would be committed voluntarily—they pray that he may be punished. For if he is not, that is, if the gods allow the High Laws to be broken with impunity, then there is no safety anywhere and no reason for religious observation. The chorus fear it is possible that the gods might cease punishing wickedness. Step by step the chorus reach, in the final antistrophe (897–910), the reason for their fear: the process of the disintegration of religion, of the gods' shirking their responsibilities, has already begun. Jocasta has just shown that the oracle about Laius' death has not come true; with this evidence the chorus can only conclude that there is grave danger that oracular pronouncements in general have ceased to be reliable. These men, who have recently had to decide that seercraft is not as reliable as they thought it was, are now forced by circumstances to another decision: "No longer will I go with reverence [i.e., belief] to the great oracular seats— Delphi, Abae, Olympia—if they are not going to give accurate predictions that suit the facts in every case. Look to this, O Zeus, for already the oracles about Laius have been proved wrong and therefore set aside; hence the worship of Apollo and indeed all religion is beginning to wane." These conclusions follow naturally from the chorus' previous attitudes about religion and the logical pattern of their reasoning as displayed in the previous scene. These practical men are not foolishly praying that Zeus will make the oracles of the past come true, but rather that he will restore the gods' credibility by preventing the utterance of false oracles in the future. Such is the sequence of ideas that the audience would most easily hear as this song proceeds.

At the same time, it has long been recognized that the listener could not possibly miss the tremendous ironies in the ode. At this point in the play, the audience has all the information needed to know that the chorus' wishes will be fulfilled, but in a way that they would never imagine or want. Somehow it will be shown that oracles will become reliable again because they never were false and that the gods will bring down *hybris*—not merely the voluntary kind that the chorus fear, but an involuntary kind that they have never imagined. The irony is particularly ingenious and terrible because it results from the general principles of religious belief, rather than mere personal joy, which the chorus espouse in all ignorance but which the audience then applies to the specific circumstances, so as to react with horror. The placing of the ode is crucial to the maintenance of the dramatic tension. The audience is surely expecting what will happen when the witness arrives. The poet must prevent the slackening of tension and the sense of anticlimax that would naturally accompany an action which the audience has been expecting; unless, of course, he deliberately fosters the audience's expectations in order to cheat them, as in the postponements of Ajax's expected suicide. It would be repetitious here for the chorus to speculate on the facts: Did Oedipus kill Laius? Will he kill his father and marry his mother? If they were, on the other hand, to condemn him or Iocasta for foolishly scoffing at oracles, the audience would simply nod in agreement and continue, perhaps with fading interest, to expect the obvious. Sophocles has therefore given the chorus a song whose ironies will generate such a feeling of horror, and pity for the chorus, that it must engage the audience's full attention and participation.

CHRISTOPHER ROCCO ON "TYRANNOS"

Sophocles considers Oedipus's "enlightened" relationship to his history, birth, and origins as a problem of fate and freedom, and introduces that problem through the figure of the tyrannos. The fifth-century tyrannos was the paradigm of the free individual—unbound by tradition, birth, history, or inherited limits. The tyrant was the man who could do and be almost anything, and who, in his escape from the past, "could become a model for human rationality and theorizing, [with] the capacity to move beyond accepted boundaries and opinions in order to imagine what was previously unimaginable, to transform the world through the power of one's mind and speech, severed from the bonds of birth and history."[16] Oedipus embodies just that combination of historical boundlessness and prideful human rationality that describes the tyrant. I have already mentioned how Oedipus solved the riddle of the Sphinx and assumed the throne of Thebes, not as hereditary *basileus* (which he in fact was), but as *tyrannos*. Yet Oedipus's attempt to escape his past, parents, and origins, and so fate, preceded his arrival at Thebes. A drunkard's insinuation about his birth first led Oedipus to Apollo's oracle (779–93), and it was the oracle's response that he, Oedipus, would murder his father and wed his mother that set him on the road to Thebes. Together with his intellectual skill, the uncertainty about his birth confers on Oedipus a sense of power, optimism, and hope, as though he could, alone and unaided, master his fate, the way he had mastered the Sphinx. When Oedipus discovers himself to be, not a child of Chance, but the accursed son of his all-too-mortal parents, Laius and Jocasta, we see before us a man with a particular history, origin, and destiny, which, no matter how hard he tries, he cannot escape, because it constitutes his very being. Watching Oedipus enlighten himself, we cannot help but recall Foucault's observation about modern disciplinary power: no matter how much in control we believe ourselves to be, forces beyond our power circumscribe our lives and direct our destinies, even as we desperately, sometimes madly, attempt to shape the forces that shape us.[17]

We should also recall, with Bernard Knox, that Oedipus's title *tyrannos* may refer, not only to the lame hero, but to Athens as well. Sophocles' Oedipus is thus "a symbolic representation of Periclean Athens," an *anthrôpos tyrannos* who resembles the *polis tyrannos* and possesses that imperial city's self-taught, self-made, and unaided ability to seize control of the environment, bending and forcing it to comply with its human designs.[18] In his role as *tyrannos*, Oedipus embodies the splendor and power of Athens: his attempt to assert dominion over nature and his unquenchable drive for human mastery; his forcefulness of purpose, his impatience, decisiveness, and daring, bordering on recklessness; his intoxication with his own accomplishments, his liberation from the constraints of all traditional pieties; his restlessness, innovation, and ingenuity; his designs that are swift alike in conception and execution, all recall the "fierce creative energy, the uncompromising logic, the initiative and daring which brought Athens to the pinnacle of worldly power."[19] To put matters this way suggests that the audience watching Oedipus also watched its own tragic power on stage.

If Knox is right about Oedipus, Athens, and the play's concern with the political context of its performance, then *Oedipus Tyrannos* is also about the Athenians' own collective self-knowledge, the limits of that knowledge, and the limits of the city's drive for empire. Through the mantic vision of the poet, the audience witnessed in "symbolic, riddling, and prophetic terms" the utter disaster immanent in Athenian intellectual and political greatness.[20] Encoded in Oedipus's name and role as *tyrannos*, then, is also the riddle of the character and fate of the Athenian citizen audience watching the play; for both "come to disaster through the valiant exercise of the very qualities that have made them great."[21]

Notes

16. Saxonhouse, "Tyranny of Reason," p. 1261. This formulation is perhaps idiosyncratic to Sophocles' play, although Thucydides does make a similar distinction between hereditary kingship (*basileia*) and tyranny, the latter characterized by rule whose privilege suffers no limits, hereditary, constitutional, or otherwise (Thucydides, *History of the Peloponnesian War* 1.13.1–17). The word *tyrannos* did not originally appear in the title of the play, but was assigned to it by tradition, perhaps as early as Aristotle; see Segal, "Sophocles." In any case, *tyrannos* underwent a series of transformations from its (probably) non-Greek origins in the seventh century, and it was not until the fourth century that it acquired a distinctly negative connotation; see A. Andrewes, *The Greek Tyrants*, 4th ed. (1956; New York: Harper & Row, 1962), pp. 28–30.

17. Michel Foucault, *Discipline and Punish: The Birth of the Prison*, trans. Alan Sheridan (1977; New York: Vintage Books, 1979), "The Carceral Archipelago."

18. Knox, *Oedipus at Thebes*, p. 107.

19. Ibid., p. 105.

20. Ibid., p. 99.

21. Ibid., p. 106. Allusion to the plague that struck Athens (and claimed the life of Pericles) shortly before Sophocles' play was produced must also be counted along with references to Pericles, Athens, and empire as evidence that Sophocles was commenting on contemporary Athens. On the relation of history to Sophoclean tragedy, see, too, Victor Ehrenberg, *Sophocles and Pericles* (Oxford: Oxford University Press, 1954).

FELIX BUDELMANN ON THE EXPANDED FOCUS OF THE PLAY

Oedipus Rex is a play firmly set in the *polis* from the prologue on. But as it proceeds, it gains a further dimension and increasingly opens out to all humankind and thus to the spectators. In the

Jocasta scene Oedipus declares that he would rather disappear unseen 'from among mortals' than be found a parricide.[58] The Chorus demand in the second stasimon that the validity of oracles be shown 'to all mortals' and in the fourth they address the 'generations of mortals' and make Oedipus their paradigm. In keeping with their stance as old men and as a generic chorus, both identities which make them appropriate commentators on human affairs, the Chorus widen the frame of reference more and more to humans in general. Membership in the large off-stage group is no longer restricted to the Thebans, but opened up to humankind at large.

This change has two notable effects. First, it does much to make the increasing concentration on Oedipus the man possible. For Thebes Oedipus is a saviour or a threat, for humans in general he is a paradigm whose thoughts and feelings may be of as much interest as his saving powers. Secondly, the widening of the large group draws in spectators. Any large group, I have suggested, invites spectators as members of a group to adopt its perspective. The difference at the end of this play is that the large group includes the spectators, whether ancient or modern, almost explicitly: they are as human as anybody.[59] Put together, this is to say that the widening out of the large group at the end of *Oedipus Rex* involves an appeal to spectators *qua* humans to look at Oedipus the paradigm.

The Thebans, I hasten to add, are of course still part of the large group. In the third stasimon the Chorus invoke Kithairon, Thebes' local mountain, and in the fourth stasimon they sing of those happy times in the past when Oedipus was honoured, 'ruling in mighty Thebes' (1203–4). More explicit[60] is something Oedipus says after all has been discovered and after he has blinded himself. As the Second Messenger reports, he requests to be shown 'all the Cadmeians' (1287–8):

He is crying for someone to unbar the gates and show to all the Cadmeians ...

Clearly, Thebes is still there. But as the Second Messenger goes on, he reaches out further (1294–6):

But he will display it to you also; for the bars of the gates are being opened, and you shall soon see such a sight as would drive to pity even one who hates him.

Spectators can refer the two addresses in these lines to themselves as much as to the Chorus or anybody else. For them, too, Oedipus is a 'sight'. And immediately after, the Chorus take up the Second Messenger with 'O grief terrible for humans to see' now explicitly reaching beyond 'the Cadmeians'. Similarly, Oedipus laments somewhat later that he is called husband of his mother by all 'mortals' and wishes he had never shown himself to 'humans'. The Thebans merge with humankind at large.

Throughout *Oedipus Rex* the Chorus offer spectators the perspective of the large group. For the most part this is the perspective of a group that is under threat and needs to be saved. None the less, the play does not tell the story of a group that is saved. Rather it tells the story of Oedipus, the chosen rescuer who gradually sheds his appointed role as he becomes caught up in the quest for his own past. Surprisingly perhaps, the result is not an open clash of interests. When Oedipus, who has effectively brought the plague upon Thebes, ends the play in misery, asking to be exiled, the Chorus are not triumphant. Throughout the play they move along with Oedipus. In the end the large group is widened out so as to include all humans as well as the Thebans, and Oedipus is looked at as a paradigm and spectacle. The group that is saved never gets a voice. Until the end the fate of Thebes remains unresolved. The changing perspective of the Chorus is one of the reasons why there are many questions to be asked about what has happened and what will happen to both Oedipus and Thebes at all points of the play, and even when it is over.

But despite the questions with which spectators are confronted, the ending of *Oedipus Rex* also yields a strange kind of comfort. Here it should become clear why I say that Sophoclean tragedy gives prominence to groups under threat but ultimately *safe*, rather than *saved*. Thebes, I just noted, is never explicitly saved, but spectators who in the beginning adopted the perspective of the group under threat can none the less feel safe now. Partly, they can feel safe because the plague, while not declared to have stopped, is at least no longer mentioned. Partly, however, they can feel safe also because almost imperceptibly the perspective of the large group has shifted. Oedipus is now a paradigm more than he is a saviour, and the large group is no longer just Thebes but incorporates all humans. Spectators watching a play are always safe in so far as they are not part of the action. They can always suffer with the characters and still retain a certain distance from their suffering. The end of *Oedipus Rex* highlights this distance and reinforces the spectators' sense of security when the perspective of the large group shifts from that of Theban citizens under threat to that of on-lookers onto a spectacle. Of course the shift is never complete. The Chorus never lose their Theban connections, just as the plague is never said to abate. But this is exactly what makes this ending so effective. Spectators, both ancient and modern, are made to ask questions at the same time as they are transported from danger to safety.

Notes

58. Cf 791–2: 'that I was destined ... to show to mortals a brood they could not bear to look on'.

59. For the inclusion of the spectators in Oedipus' audience at the end of the play see Segal (1993) 27–9.

60. Note also the tailpiece which is addressed to the 'dwellers in our native land of Thebes' (1524). There is, however, a strong possibility that these lines are spurious: p. 210, n. 34 above.

ALAN H. SOMMERSTEIN ON THE WORLD OF SOPHOCLES

The universe that Sophocles portrays is one that has an awesome and far-reaching logic. This logic is perceptible in the regular, inexorable cycles of nature, of which Ajax speaks and the women of Trachis sing; in the equally inexorable fulfilment of prophecies and oracles, often by devious and unexpected paths; in the repeated motif, mentioned above, of the dead destroying the living; and in various small symmetries and coincidences—as when Ajax kills himself with the sword Hector had given him, after Hector had been dragged to his death by the belt Ajax had given *him*; or when the prayers of Iocaste and Clytaemestra to Apollo are each instantly answered by the arrival of a messenger with news which seems to be exactly what they had hoped for, but which in fact leads to the destruction of them both. In general, however, and in contrast with Aeschylus, it is not a logic that is agreeable either to our morality or to that of classical Athenians. For example, as Sophocles shapes the story of Oedipus, the actions of all those involved, from Oedipus himself to the two shepherds, which between them led to the catastrophe that happens in *Oedipus the King*, were all reasonable in the circumstances, and many of them were thoroughly praiseworthy. Again, Philoctetes suffers ten years of agony for a minor, and apparently inadvertent, act of sacrilege; it is true that the Atreidae and Odysseus, by abandoning him on Lemnos instead of taking him home, make his sufferings even worse, but we gather that whatever had happened his wound could be healed only at Troy and only in the tenth year. The gods, it seems, have their ways and their plans, and if human lives get in the way of these then human lives may be wrecked. The bleakness of this outlook is mitigated in three ways. In the first place, we are allowed to glimpse something of the grand logic by which these plans are governed: we cannot fully comprehend it, but we can at least see that it has its own cruel beauty. As a corollary of this, Sophocles never in the surviving plays shows gods in conflict with one another: either the gods are thought of as a collectivity, or else only one of them (Zeus, Apollo, Athena) is portrayed as active in a given story. Secondly, even if suffering is not always *caused* by wrongdoing, its major victims tend to be shown committing wrongs which for a theatre audience, if not for a philosophical observer, considerably mitigate any sense of injustice—the tyrannical behaviour of Creon and of Oedipus, the treatment by Heracles of the people of Oechalia, of Lichas, and of his wife; in *Philoctetes*, where the major victim is completely innocent, he is splendidly recompensed and his chief tormentor disgraced. And thirdly (and related to this), Sophocles' choruses and characters frequently encourage us to reflect on the uncertainties of life, the constant possibility of reversals of fortune, and the danger that success may lead to arrogance. Awareness of these things is one aspect of the virtue that Greeks called *sôphrosynê*. The trouble is that in general, he who is *sôphrôn* is not likely to be a person of great achievement, and vice versa; but such a combination is nevertheless possible, as witness Odysseus in *Ajax* and Theseus in *Oedipus at Colonus*— and indeed Neoptolemus, once he has shaken off the influence of his play's very different version of Odysseus.

Sophocles' plays do not normally bear any direct relation to specific contemporary events, but in a broader sense most of them are highly relevant to the public concerns of a *polis* community. *Antigone* explores the meaning and limits of the citizen's duty of obedience to law and authority and of the Athenian's oath of allegiance. The responsibilities of leaders, military and political, to those whom they lead, are as much a theme of *Ajax* or *Oedipus the King* as of *Seven against Thebes* or *The Persians*. *Philoctetes* taps into the great debates of the late fifth century on the social education of the young, and on whether political ends justify means. There are no easy answers; there never are. Communities need leaders of intelligence and resolution; yet to put all one's trust in one's intelligence, to persevere unshakably in one's resolution, are perilous for the individual and may themselves endanger the community. The contrast between the virtuous democratic community and the arrogant, selfish leader is much less prominent in Sophocles than in Aeschylus; the tendency in Sophocles is rather to emphasize the *dependence* of the community on their leader's guidance and protection. In his two Trojan War plays, the choruses are portrayed not as soldiers but as (unarmed, poor) sailors; the Thebans look to Oedipus almost as a god; in *Antigone* the public oppose Creon's edict but are apparently paralysed by fear; in *Oedipus at Colonus* the villagers of Colonus can take neither decision nor action without Theseus. Aeschylus died when the radical Athenian democracy was only five or six years old. Sophocles lived in it for another half century and came to know its weaknesses as well as its strengths: that while 'a *polis* that belongs to one man is no true *polis*' (*Antigone*, line 737), nevertheless 'the little without the great are a frail protection for a fortress: the small are best supported by the great, and the great by the lesser' (*Ajax*, lines 158–161).

Works by Sophocles

Ajax, c. 447 B.C.

Antigone, c. 442 B.C.

Ichneutai, c. 440 B.C. (the satyr play).

Oedipus the King, c. 430 B.C.

Electra, c. 418–414 B.C.

The Women of Trachis, c. 413 B.C.

Philoctetes, 409 B.C.

Oedipus at Colonus, produced posthumously in 401 B.C.

Annotated Bibliography

Ahl, Frederick. *Sophocles' Oedipus: Evidence and Self-Conviction.* Ithaca and London: Cornell University Press, 1991.

Ahl's book is written for the student who is interested in Greek tragedy but lacks specialized knowledge. Ahl focuses on some of the most perplexing questions raised by the play and encourages multiple readings and interpretations. He gives an extensive analysis to each scene in *Oedipus Rex*. Differences in translations are also considered. This book is highly readable and engaging.

Bowra, C. W. *Sophoclean Tragedy.* Oxford: Clarendon Press, 1944.

C. M. Bowra states at the outset his intention to focus on the ideas of the plays rather than on their poetic qualities or other technical aspects. The ideas discussed are profound but not difficult to follow. A chapter is devoted to each play.

Budelmann, Felix. *The Language of Sophocles: Communality, Communication, and Involvement.* Cambridge: Cambridge University Press, 2000.

Budelmann traces Sophoclean criticism over the years, noting that studies of Sophocles are becoming more specialized. Budelmann focuses on commonality among the different responses to Sophoclean language over the centuries. In particular, he notices a fascination with ambiguity.

Burton, R. W. B. *Sophocles' Tragedies.* Oxford: Clarendon Press, 1980.

Burton believes the role of the chorus in Sophoclean tragedy has received less attention than it deserves. Before giving a highly detailed and specialized reading of the chorus in each of Sophocles' seven extant plays, Burton discusses the multiple purposes the chorus may serve for the artist. These include highlighting events from the past, creating audience response to a specific actor or event onstage, summarizing earlier scenes, and reflecting on the meaning of an event.

The author's chapter on *Oedipus Rex* demonstrates the range of emotions expressed by the chorus in this play—sometimes speaking with one voice, sometimes presenting contradictory views, as would be expected of a random grouping of Athenian citizens. A line-by-line analysis follows closely the subtle changes in attitude the chorus experiences as the king falls from fortune and grace to ruin and banishment. A knowledge of Greek is helpful for readers of this book but not essential; the author sometimes quotes the original Greek without providing a translation.

Collins, Clifton W. *Ancient Classics for English Readers: Sophocles.* Philadelphia: J. B. Lippincott & Co., 1875.

This study of Sophocles written more than a century ago is interesting for the similarities of insight and concern between then and now. The introduction provides the scant biographical information on Sophocles available in 1875 (somewhat more has been discovered since then); a chapter is devoted to each of the plays.

Foley, Helene P. *Female Acts in Greek Tragedy.* Princeton and Oxford: Princeton University Press, 2001.

Other than observing Jocasta's enactment of the traditional female role when she intervenes to calm the family argument between husband and brother, this study of women as actors in Greek tragedy does not have much commentary on *Oedipus Rex*. However, Foley's discussions of Homer's Penelope, Sophocles' Antigone and Electra, and Euripides' Medea are illuminating and original.

Gardiner, Cynthia P. *The Sophoclean Chorus: A Study of Character and Function.* Iowa City: University of Iowa Press, 1987.

Gardiner focuses less on technicalities than on the chorus's presence as an actor in its own right in the play. In the section on *Oedipus Rex*, Gardiner follows the interactions between the chorus and other characters and observes that such interaction helps develop the characters.

Jebb, R. C. *Sophocles: Plays—"Oedipus Tyrannus."* Eds. P. E. Easterling and Jeffrey Rusten. London: Bristol Classical Press, 2004.

This volume is among the most extensive and scholarly of the works recently published on the play. R. C. Jebb was the most revered British hellenist of his time (he died in 1905). His translations and commentaries on the plays of Sophocles have been so popular that copies have literally faded away from overuse or disappeared into private libraries. The editors have added to this exact reproduction of the original work published in 1893 some commentary that affords a historical perspective on enduring reader responses. Jebb's translations are printed on one side of each page with the corresponding Greek on the other side. The original commentary is included. A large section explaining the metrical patterns is another feature. This study is required reading for the advanced student but is interestingly presented for the general student as well.

Kitto, H. D. F. *Sophocles: Dramatist and Philospher*. London: Oxford University Press, 1958.

This little book, consisting of three lectures given by Professor Kitto, combines wisdom and common sense in discussing the ancient and still-relevant issues raised by Sophocles. Kitto shows that Sophocles was a profound thinker as well as a brilliant dramatist. His lectures are so engaging and accessible the reader may forget that he or she is not actually in the audience.

Leinieks, Valdis. *The Plays of Sophokles*. Amsterdam: B. R. Gruner Publishing Co., 1982.

This study of Sophocles devotes a chapter to each of the seven plays and draws the reader into a line-by-line and section-by-section analysis of the ideas embedded in the text. Much reverence is expressed for the limits of our understanding, and variations of interpretations are emphasized.

Meineck, Peter, and Paul Woodruff. *Sophocles: The Theban Plays.* Indianapolis and Cambridge: Hackett Publishing Company, Inc., 2003.

This volume includes new translations by the authors of Sophocles' Theban plays. Easily accessible footnotes accompany the lines where ambiguities in translations make for ambiguities of understanding.

The introduction provides biographical and performance information. The authors acknowledge a deep affection for these plays and occasionally offer personal responses—an interesting addition not commonly found in academic works.

Pedrick, Victoria, and Steven M. Oberhelman, eds. *The Soul of Tragedy: Essays on Athenian Drama.* Chicago and London: University of Chicago Press, 2005.

This recent book brings together diverse scholars to attempt a comprehensive picture of ancient Athenian culture, using newer paradigms of thought, including the psychoanalytic. The volume contains several discussions about the Greek attitude toward women. The content is sophisticated and requires considerable prior knowledge of the subject.

Scodel, Ruth. *Sophocles.* Boston: Twayne Publishers, 1984.

Scodel's study of Sophocles is an excellent discussion for students of Greek tragedy. She devotes a chapter to each play, emphasizing a particular issue such as fate, guilt, and the limits of human understanding.

Her discussions are profound and accessible at the same time. A final chapter on the achievement of Sophocles contains many interesting details, including the history of safeguarding and reprinting the plays that we have so readily available to us now.

Seale, David. *Vision and Stagecraft in Sophocles.* London: Croom Helm Ltd., 1982.

Seale's study of Sophocles concentrates on the theatrical presentation of the plays. Countering a prevailing view of

Sophocles as an artist less spectacular in stage presentation than Aeschylus or Euripides, Seale looks at each of the plays to demonstrate Sophocles' talent for creating spectacle with meaning.

Whitman, Cedric H. *The Heroic Paradox: Essays on Homer, Sophocles, and Aristophanes.* Ithaca and London: Cornell University Press, 1982.

Whitman's book is another accessible study of Greek literature and ideas. The author assumes, however, that his readers are willing to ponder philosophical and metaphysical ideas often not at all easy to grasp. Particularly helpful is the author's lengthy and far-ranging effort to define "heroic" and "tragic"—both words commonly misused and misunderstood.

Zimmermann, Bernhard. *Greek Tragedy: An Introduction.* trans. Thomas Marier. Baltimore and London: Johns Hopkins University Press, 1991.

As befits a book offering an introduction, Zimmermann's *Greek Tragedy* provides a clear and inviting entry to the study of the three best-known Greek tragic dramatists. A section apiece is devoted to Aeschylus, Sophocles, and Euripides with some biographical material and commentary on selected works. The introduction is a mix of straightforward and complex discussion of such features as meter, music, political connections, and the function of the chorus.

 Contributors

Harold Bloom is Sterling Professor of the Humanities at Yale University. He is the author of 30 books, including *Shelley's Mythmaking, The Visionary Company, Blake's Apocalypse, Yeats, A Map of Misreading, Kabbalah and Criticism, Agon: Toward a Theory of Revisionism, The American Religion, The Western Canon,* and *Omens of Millennium: The Gnosis of Angels, Dreams, and Resurrection. The Anxiety of Influence* sets forth Professor Bloom's provocative theory of the literary relationships between the great writers and their predecessors. His most recent books include *Shakespeare: The Invention of the Human,* a 1998 National Book Award finalist; *How to Read and Why; Genius: A Mosaic of One Hundred Exemplary Creative Minds; Hamlet: Poem Unlimited; Where Shall Wisdom Be Found?;* and *Jesus and Yahweh: The Names Divine.* In 1999, Professor Bloom received the prestigious American Academy of Arts and Letters Gold Medal for Criticism. He has also received the International Prize of Catalonia, the Alfonso Reyes Prize of Mexico, and the Hans Christian Andersen Bicentennial Prize of Denmark.

Camille-Yvette Welsch teaches at the Pennsylvania State University. She is a poet and critic whose work has appeared in *Mid-American Review, The AWP Writer's Chronicle, The Women's Review of Books, Barrow Street,* and *Small Spiral Notebook,* among other venues.

Clifton W. Collins served as Her Majesty's Inspector of Schools.

C. M. Bowra (Sir Maurice) taught at Oxford. He also wrote about Homer, Pindar, and Sophocles.

H. D. F. Kitto was professor of Greek at the University of Bristol. His works include *Greek Tragedy: A Literary Study* (1939); *The Greeks* (1951); and *Form and Meaning in Drama: A Study of Six Plays and of Hamlet* (1956).

Bernard M. W. Knox has served as Director of the Center for Hellenistic Studies in Washington, D.C. He has written extensively on Greek culture and literature. In 1985 he coedited *Greek Literature* with P. E. Easterling. Other works include *Oedipus at Thebes* (1957), *The Heroic Temper: Studies in Sophoclean Tragedy* (1964), *Essays Ancient and Modern* (1989), and *Backing into the Future: The Classical Tradition and Its Renewal* (1994).

E. R. Dodds was Regius Professor of Greek at Oxford. He wrote *The Greeks and the Irrational* (1957) and *The Ancient Concept of Progress and Other Essays on Greek Literature and Belief* (1973).

Herbert Musurillo was the editor of *The Acts of the Pagan Martyrs: Acta Alexandrinorum* (1954). In addition to *The Light and the Darkness: Studies in the Dramatic Poetry of Sophocles* (1967), Herbert Musurillo translated and wrote the introduction for *Acts of the Christian Martyrs* (1972) and translated, edited, and wrote commentary for *Acts of the Pagan Martyrs* (2000).

David Seale wrote *Vision and Stagecraft in Sophocles* in 1982.

Cynthia P. Gardiner wrote *The Sophoclean Chorus: A Study of Character and Function* (1987).

Christopher Rocco teaches in the Political Science Department at the University of Connecticut. He wrote *Tragedy and Enlightenment: Athenian Political Thought and the Dilemmas of Modernity* (1997).

Felix Budelmann is a lecturer in Greek at the University of Manchester.

Alan H. Sommerstein is professor of Greek at the University of Nottingham. He has served as the director of the Centre for Ancient Drama and Its Reception. In addition to his work on Sophocles he has translated and written about Aeschylus and Aristophanes.

Acknowledgments

Collins, Clifton W. "Introduction." *Ancient Classics for English Readers: Sophocles.* J. B. Lippincott & Co., 1875, pp. 9–13.

Bowra, C. M. "The Nature of the Subject." *Sophoclean Tragedy.* Clarendon Press, 1944, pp. 1–16. Reprinted with permission.

Kitto, H. D. F. "Human and Divine Drama." *Sophocles: Dramatist and Philosopher.* London: Oxford University Press, 1958, pp. 47–50.

Knox, Bernard M. W. "Hero." *Oedipus at Thebes.* New Haven, Conn.: Yale University Press, 1957, pp. 185–96, 265–66. Reprinted by permission of Yale University Press.

Dodds, E. R. "On Misunderstanding the *Oedipus Rex*" *Twentieth Century Views of "Oedipus Rex": A Collection of Critical Essays: Oedipus Rex.* Michael J. O'Brien, ed. Englewood Cliffs, N.J: Prentice-Hall, Inc.,1966, pp.17–29.

Musurillo, Herbert. "Blindness and Vision: *Oedipus Tyrannus.*" *The Light and The Darkness: Studies in the Dramatic Poetry of Sophocles.* Leiden: E. J. Brill, 1967, pp. 82–85.

Seale, David. "*Oedipus the King*: Blindness and Sight." *Vision and Stagecraft in Sophocles.* Chicago: University of Chicago Press, 1982, pp. 215–16. Reprinted by permission of The University of Chicago Press.

Gardiner, Cynthia P. "*Antigone, Oedipus Tyrannus, Oedipus Coloneus.*" *The Sophoclean Chorus: A Study of Character and Function.* Iowa City: University of Iowa Press, 1987, pp. 104–106.

Rocco, Christopher. "Sophocles' *Oedipus Tyrannos:* The Tragedy of Enlightenment." *Tragedy and Enlightenment: Athenian*

Political Thought and the Dilemmas of Modernity. Berkeley: University of California Press, 1997, pp. 40–42. Reprinted by permission.

Budelmann, Felix. "The Chorus: Shared Survival." *The Language of Sophocles: Communality, Communication and Involvement*. Cambridge: Cambridge University Press, 2000, pp. 228–31. Reprinted with the permission of Cambridge University Press.

Sommerstein, Alan H. "The Authors: Sophocles." *Greek Drama and Dramatists*. New York: Thomson Publishing Services, Copyright © 2002, pp. 46–48. Reproduced by permission of Taylor and Francis Books UK.

Index

Characters in literary works are indexed by first name (if any), followed by the name of the work in parentheses.